AMERIFIL.TXT

Poets on Poetry

DAVID LEHMAN, GENERAL EDITOR

A. R. Ammons *Set in Motion*
Douglas Crase *AMERIFIL.TXT*
Suzanne Gardinier *A World That Will Hold All the People*
Kenneth Koch *The Art of Poetry*

DONALD HALL, FOUNDING EDITOR

Martin Lammon, Editor
  Written in Water, Written in Stone
Philip Booth *Trying to Say It*
Joy Harjo *The Spiral of Memory*
Richard Tillinghast
  Robert Lowell's Life and Work
Marianne Boruch *Poetry's Old Air*
Alan Williamson *Eloquence and Mere Life*
Mary Kinzie *The Judge Is Fury*
Thom Gunn *Shelf Life*
Robert Creeley *Tales Out of School*
Fred Chappell *Plow Naked*
Gregory Orr *Richer Entanglements*
Daniel Hoffman *Words to Create a World*
David Lehman *The Line Forms Here*
  · *The Big Question*
Jane Miller *Working Time*
Amy Clampitt *Predecessors, Et Cetera*
Peter Davison
  One of the Dangerous Trades
William Meredith
  Poems Are Hard to Read
Tom Clark *The Poetry Beat*
William Matthews *Curiosities*
Charles Wright *Halflife* · *Quarter Notes*
Weldon Kees
  Reviews and Essays, 1936–55
Tess Gallagher *A Concert of Tenses*
Charles Simic *The Uncertain Certainty*
  · *Wonderful Words, Silent Truth*
  · *The Unemployed Fortune-Teller*
Anne Sexton *No Evil Star*
John Frederick Nims *A Local Habitation*

Donald Justice *Platonic Scripts*
Robert Hayden *Collected Prose*
Hayden Carruth *Effluences from the
  Sacred Caves* · *Suicides and Jazzers*
John Logan *A Ballet for the Ear*
Alicia Ostriker
  Writing Like a Woman
Marvin Bell *Old Snow Just Melting*
James Wright *Collected Prose*
Marge Piercy
  Parti-Colored Blocks for a Quilt
John Haines *Living Off the Country*
Philip Levine *Don't Ask*
Louis Simpson *A Company of Poets*
  · *The Character of the Poet*
  · *Ships Going into the Blue*
Richard Kostelanetz
  The Old Poetries and the New
David Ignatow *Open Between Us*
Robert Francis *Pot Shots at Poetry*
Robert Bly *Talking All Morning*
Diane Wakoski *Toward a New Poetry*
Maxine Kumin *To Make a Prairie*
Donald Davie *Trying to Explain*
William Stafford
  Writing the Australian Crawl ·
  You Must Revise Your Life
Galway Kinnell
  Walking Down the Stairs
Donald Hall *Goatfoot Milktongue
  Twinbird* · *The Weather for Poetry
  Poetry and Ambition* · *Death to the
  Death of Poetry*

Douglas Crase

AMERIFIL.TXT

A Commonplace Book

Ann Arbor
THE UNIVERSITY OF MICHIGAN PRESS

Copyright © by the University of Michigan 1996
All rights reserved
Published in the United States of America by
The University of Michigan Press
Printed and bound by CPI Group (UK) Ltd, Croydon, CR0 4YY

1999   1998   1997   1996   4   3   2   1

*A CIP catalog record for this book is available
from the British Library.*

Library of Congress Cataloging-in-Publication Data

AMERIFIL.TXT : a commonplace book / [compiled by] Douglas Crase.
     p.   cm. —(Poets on poetry)
   Includes index.
   ISBN 978-0-472-09636-7 (hardcover : alk. paper). — ISBN 978-0-472-06636-0
(pbk. : alk. paper)
   1. Quotations, American.   2. Commonplace-books   I. Crase,
Douglas.   II. Series.
PN6244.A45   1997
818'.02—dc20   96-30227
                                                          CIP

To Brian Walker

Preface

Love, Emerson wrote, is "the bright foreigner," and whether this comes true metaphorically or true in fact, sooner or later you may show that foreigner your home. Perhaps you won't have to go there. Perhaps, if you live in North America, home is increasingly hard to find. In trade talks, the French have refused free entry to feature films on the theory that, overrun by American movies, France may be hard to find. Everybody likes to think industrialized entertainment is American. A columnist hired on as host of a television series and defended his new job by remarking that if you are not on television you are not an American. At Kodak, the managers used to observe that an American was anybody defined by certain inalienable rights, to drive a car and to take a picture. The jokes reveal that the characteristics in question are not so unique to anybody as they are advantageous to those who want every last everybody to require, from birth, their products. Homespun would create the unavailable market, which is why homespun was worn by the American resistance during the Revolution.

A commonplace book might serve as a map of home. When I began this one I made rules, therefore, to keep it faithful to its origins. First was to limit its entries to writers that truly had claimed me, not those I wished since to claim, but those whose words had arrived uninterruptably once as fate, or puberty. It does not seem remarkable to me if, for an American, such writers should be American. It seems remarkable it could be any other way.

Most of these writers are poets. Others are part, in retrospect, of poetry's own terms. Some, in a tradition by which the Americas themselves are the greatest poem, are poets we know as naturalists instead. One of the pieties is that art anticipates attitudes. Yet the naturalists represented here were contemporaries in turn of certain poets whose outlooks now seem, by comparison, social history.

The quotations come only from books I could find in the house. They were democratically available, I wanted to think, to anyone that reads. They had to have staying power, proved by an address in memory. In books of mine, this meant they were marked or underlined. No quote was allowed from a work by which its author is best known. If the writers are poets, I did not quote from their poems. If the writers are known for prose, I did not quote from their masterworks, only from journals or letters, lectures or reviews. When even these seemed sufficiently famous, as Emerson's journals presently do, I tightened the rule to avoid the popular excerpts. And when, in the case of *Democratic Vistas*, it seemed livelier never to have made the rule, I broke it. In arranging the entries, I tried to honor a precedent set by the writers themselves: Explanation forecloses surprise, and surprise is the one way that reading can be as powerful as, or even become, experience.

Many entries are in the public domain. Others are from work still under copyright. Each is quoted in fair use, and none in a way to make its source superfluous. I include the citations in thanks to publishers and in fairness to authors, but mainly in tribute to friends and foreigners who are entitled to remake this territory as their own.

D. C.

Contents

Anxiety of Influence

The United States is just now the oldest country in the world, there always is an oldest country and she is it, it is she who is the mother of the twentieth century civilization. She began to feel herself as it just after the Civil War. And so it is a country the right age to have been born in and the wrong age to live in. . . . Your parent's home is never a place to work it is a nice place to be brought up in. Later on there will be place enough to get away from home in the United States, it is beginning, then there will be creators who live at home.

Gertrude Stein

As an adolescent, the thing I most seriously wanted to be was an architect. Although I had no particular gift in that direction, I was a fan of Frank Lloyd Wright. But reading is what I did most of, poetry and prose. In the back of our house was a gully, a slightly wild area, where I had a tent for the summer. And I was reading a book called *Unforgotten Years*, by Logan Pearsall Smith. He told how Whitman used to come to their house in Philadelphia from Camden, and what it was like— how Whitman used to sit in the outhouse singing "Old Jim Crow." But then he says the idea suddenly entered his mind that maybe someday he, too, could be a writer. And I looked up from the book to the landscape outside, and it all sort of shimmered.

James Schuyler

It was like throwing a million bricks out of my heart—for it wasn't only the books that I wanted to throw away, but every thing miserable and unpleasant out of my past: the memory of my father, the poverty and uncertainties of my mother's life, the stupidities of color-prejudice, black in a white world, the fear of not finding a job, the bewilderment of no one to talk to about things that trouble you, the feeling of always being controlled by others—by parents, by employers, by some outer necessity not your own. All those things I wanted to throw away.

Langston Hughes

Now, when all the primitive difficulties of getting started have been overcome, we live in the tradition which is the true mythology of the region and we breathe in with every breath the joy of having ourselves been created by what has been endured and mastered in the past.

Wallace Stevens

One book only did Hughes save. He had flung overboard the symbols of his hurt. . . . He saved his copy of Walt Whitman's Leaves of Grass.

I had no intention of throwing that one away.

Langston Hughes

The Art of Losing

To be worthy of what we lose is the supreme Aim—

Emily Dickinson

As Big as You Please

And also, from hence gather and go home with this meditation: that certainly here is this distemper in our natures, that we cannot tell how to use liberty, but shall very readily corrupt ourselves. Oh, the bottomless depth of sandy earth! of a corrupt spirit, that breaks over all bounds, and loves inordinate vastness! That is it we ought to be careful of.

John Cotton

My wickedness, as I am in myself, has long appeared to me perfectly ineffable and infinitely swallowing up all thought and imagination, like an infinite deluge or infinite mountains over my head. I know not how to express better what my sins appear to me to be than by heaping infinite upon infinite, and multiplying infinite by infinite. I go about very often, for this many years, with these expressions in my mind and in my mouth, "Infinite upon infinite. Infinite upon infinite!" When

I look into my heart and take a view of my wickedness, it looks like an abyss infinitely deeper than hell. And it appears to me that were it not for free grace, exalted and raised up to the infinite height of all the fullness and glory of the great Jehovah, and the arm of His power and grace stretched forth, in all the majesty of His power and in all the glory of His sovereignty, I should appear sunk down in my sins infinitely below hell itself, far beyond sight of everything but the piercing eye of God's grace, that can pierce even down to such a depth and to the bottom of such an abyss.

Jonathan Edwards

In all my lectures, I have taught one doctrine, namely, the infinitude of the private man.

Ralph Waldo Emerson

Being a Genius

It is not possible to prepare for a crisis in the middle of a crisis. To start a large turbine you cannot throw steam into the drum; the inertia is too great; you run it by means of a small engine until it has been stepped up to the point at which steam can be added.

Marianne Moore

It takes a lot of time to be a genius, you have to sit around so much doing nothing really doing nothing. If a bird or birds fly into the room is it good luck or bad luck we will say it is good luck.

Gertrude Stein

Look sharply after your thoughts. They come unlooked for, like a new bird seen on your trees, and, if you turn to your usual task, disappear; and you shall never find that perception again; never, I say,—but perhaps years, ages, and I know not what events and worlds may lie between you and its return!

Ralph Waldo Emerson

One never knows of course. Very often there isn't anything there but you have to proceed on the assumption that something is, otherwise you don't write.

John Ashbery

The neologisms of talk in one's sleep or half-sleep are not nearly so worthwhile as the acceleration and definition of ideas when one lies awake early in the morning, say, after a thoroughly good night's rest. How often when one has been trying to say something in one's room during the evening and when one has not even been sure what it was that one wanted to say, things come to mind with all the force of acute concentration as one sits on the edge of the bed wishing that it wasn't true that Guinness sells 25,000 barrels of stout a week (or a month) in the South of Ireland alone, or something equally irrelevant. Of course that common enough experience is actually an episode of concentration, so that after a bit one comes to recognize that it is not exceptional, like a blandishment on the part of a fat and happy muse, but that it is an elevation available at will.

Wallace Stevens

Results should not be too voluntarily aimed at or too busily thought of. They are *sure* to float up of their own accord, from a long enough daily work at a given matter.

William James

Q: Did you awake to it, "or was your arrival at prominence gradual?"

A: Gradual—very gradual—quite long, slow and gradual. In fact, it was so gradual that I got tired.

Langston Hughes

The Body Electric

It occurred to me when I awoke this morning, feeling regret for intemperance of the day before in eating fruit, which had dulled my sensibilities, that man was to be treated as a musical instrument, and if any viol was to be made of sound timber and kept well tuned always, it was he, so that when the bow of events is drawn across him he may vibrate and resound in perfect harmony. A sensitive soul will be continually trying its strings to see if they are in tune. A man's body must be rasped down exactly to a shaving. It is of far more importance than the wood of a Cremona violin.

Henry David Thoreau

I am glad if Theodore balked the Professors—Most such are Manikins, and a warm blow from a brave Anatomy, hurls them into Wherefores—

Emily Dickinson

Captivity Narrative

Our philosophy is to *wait*. We have retreated on patience, transferring our oft shattered hope now to larger & eternal good. We meant well, but our uncle was crazy & must be restrained from waking the house. The roof leaked, we were out of wood, our sisters were unmarried & must be maintained; there were taxes to pay, & notes, and, alas, a tomb to build: we were pledged continually to postpone our best action, and that which was life to do, could only be smuggled in to odd moments of the month & year.

Ralph Waldo Emerson

The Common Defense

Hitler and Germany can be smashed of course, after years; but I wonder whether anyone realizes what the state of Europe and the world will be by that time? Even if those "four freedoms" were to be honestly established at a peace conference, nobody but the U.S. could enforce them; and we shall

never be Roman nor German enough to police the world for a
long time. And if we did—could this be called freedom?

Robinson Jeffers

Has the Mexican war terminated yet & how? Are we beat? Do
you know of any nation about to besiege South Hadley? If so,
do inform me of it, for I would be glad of a chance to escape,
if we are to be stormed.

Emily Dickinson

The whole present system of the officering and personnel of
the army and navy of these States, and the spirit and letter of
their trebly-aristocratic rules and regulations, is a monstrous
exotic, a nuisance and revolt, and belong here just as much as
orders of nobility, or the Pope's council of cardinals. I say if
the present theory of our army and navy is sensible and true,
then the rest of America is an unmitigated fraud.

Walt Whitman

That evening I went over to talk to the soldiers, and to hear
what they had to say, we all got very excited, Sergeant
Santiani who had asked me to come complained that I con-
fused the minds of his men but why shouldn't their minds be
confused, gracious goodness, are we going to be like the
Germans, only believe in the Aryans that is our own race, a
mixed race if you like but all having the same point of view. I
got very angry with them, they admitted they like the Ger-
mans better than the other Europeans. Of course you do, I
said, they flatter you and obey you, when the other countries
don't like you and say so and personally you have not been
awfully ready to meet them half way, well naturally if they
don't like you they show it, the Germans don't like you but
they flatter you, doggone it, I said I bet you Fourth of July
they will all be putting up our flag and all you big babies will
just be flattered to death, literally to death, because you will
have to fight again. Well said one of them after all we are on
top. Yes I said and is there any spot on earth more danger-

ous than on top. You don't like the Latins, or the Arabs or the Wops, or the British, well don't you forget a country can't live without friends, I want you all to get to understand other countries so that you can be friends, make a little effort, try to find out what it is all about. We got very excited, they passed me cognac, but I don't drink so they found me some grapefruit juice, and they patted me and sat me down, and there it all was.

Gertrude Stein

There can be no thought of escape. Both the poet and the mystic may establish themselves on herrings and apples. The painter may establish himself on a guitar, a copy of *Figaro* and a dish of melons. These are fortifyings, although irrational ones. The only possible resistance to the pressure of the contemporaneous is a matter of herrings and apples or, to be less definite, the contemporaneous itself. In poetry, to that extent, the subject is not the contemporaneous, because that is only the nominal subject, but the poetry of the contemporaneous. Resistance to the pressure of ominous and destructive circumstance consists of its conversion, so far as possible, into a different, an explicable, an amenable circumstance.

Wallace Stevens

Communion of Saints

We cannot wonder at the aversion with which old bachelors and old maids have been regarded. Marriage is the natural means of forming a sphere, of taking root on the earth: it requires more strength to do this without such an opening, very many have failed to this, and their imperfections have been in every one's way. . . . Yet the business of society has become so complex, that it could now scarcely be carried on without the presence of these despised auxiliaries, and detachments from the army of aunts and uncles are wanted to stop gaps in every hedge.

Margaret Fuller

Many will say it is a dream, and will not follow my inferences: but I confidently expect a time when there will be seen, running like a half-hid warp through all the myriad audible and visible worldly interests of America, threads of manly friendship, fond and loving, pure and sweet, strong and life-long, carried to degrees hitherto unknown—not only giving tone to individual character, and making it unprecedently emotional, muscular, heroic, and refined, but having the deepest relations to general politics. I say democracy infers such loving comradeship, as its most inevitable twin or counterpart, without which it will be incomplete, in vain, and incapable of perpetuating itself.

Walt Whitman

The loveliest sermon I ever heard was the disappointment of Jesus in Judas. It was told like a mortal story of intimate young men.

Emily Dickinson

Saints II

Do we not already sing our love for and obligation to the land of the free and the home of the brave? Yes, but just what and whom do we love? Certainly not the soil, which we are sending helter-skelter downriver. Certainly not the waters, which we assume have no function except to turn turbines, float barges, and carry off sewage. Certainly not the plants, of which we exterminate whole communities without batting an eye. Certainly not the animals of which we have already extirpated many of the largest and most beautiful species. A land ethic of course cannot prevent the alteration, management, and use of these "resources," but it does affirm their right to continued existence, and, at least in spots, their continued existence in a natural state.

Aldo Leopold

Comparative Literature

Gertrude Stein, b. 1874
Rainer Maria Rilke, b. 1875

The Conduct of Life

Does Wisdom work in a tread-mill? or does she teach how to succeed *by her example*? Is there any such thing as wisdom not applied to life? Is she merely the miller who grinds the finest logic? It is pertinent to ask if Plato got his *living* in a better way or more successfully than his contemporaries,—or did he succumb to the difficulties of life like other men? Did he seem to prevail over some of them merely by indifference, or by assuming grand airs? or find it easier to live, merely because his aunt remembered him in her will? The ways in which most men get their living, that is, live, are mere makeshifts, and a shirking of the real business of life,—chiefly because they do not know, but partly because they do not mean, any better.

Henry David Thoreau

Consent of the Governed

I don't envisage collectivism. There is no such animal, it is always individualism, sometimes the rest vote and sometimes they do not, and if they do they do and if they do not they do not.

Gertrude Stein

Not a man faces round at the rest with terrible negative voice, refusing all terms to be bought off from his own eye-sight, or from the soul that he is, or from friendship, or from the body that he is, or from the soil and sea. To creeds, literature, art, the army, the navy, the executive, life is hardly proposed, but the sick and dying are proposed to cure the sick and dying. The churches are one vast lie; the people do not believe them, and they do not believe themselves; the priests are continually telling what they know well enough is not so, and keeping back what they know is so. The spectacle is a pitiful one. I think there can never be again upon the festive earth more bad-disordered persons deliberately taking seats, as of late in These States, at the heads of the public tables—such corpses' eyes for judges—such a rascal and thief in the Presidency.

Walt Whitman

The Leaves are flying high away, and the Heart flies with them, though where that wondrous Firm alight, is not "an open secret—" What a curious Lie that phrase is! I see it of Politicians—Before I write to you again, we shall have had a new Czar—

Emily Dickinson

The Creation

We live in a scientific age; yet we assume that knowledge of science is the prerogative of only a small number of human beings, isolated and priestlike in their laboratories. This is not true. The materials of science are the materials of life itself.

Rachel Carson

If we knew more chemistry and physics I'd have more faith.

Lorine Niedecker

Science will not trust us with another World.

Emily Dickinson

Credits

John Wise (1652–1725)
    No other American colonial author equals John Wise in breadth and power of thought.

Thomas Jefferson

Jonathan Edwards (1703–1758)
Few bodies or parties have served the world so well as the Puritans. . . . Franklin is such a fruit as might be expected from such a tree. Edwards, perhaps more so.

Ralph Waldo Emerson

Ralph Waldo Emerson (1803–1882)
I was simmering, simmering, simmering; Emerson brought me to a boil.

Walt Whitman

The reading of the divine Emerson, volume after volume, has done me a lot of good, and, strange to say, has thrown a strong practical light on my own path.

William James

With the Kingdom of Heaven on his knee, could Mr Emerson hesitate?

Emily Dickinson

Margaret Fuller (1810–1850)
Margaret Fuller talking of Women, said, "Who would be a goody that could be a genius?"

Ralph Waldo Emerson

Henry David Thoreau (1817–1862)
As for taking T.'s arm, I should as soon take the arm of an elm tree.

Ralph Waldo Emerson

Walt Whitman (1819–1892)
Dramatic unities; laws of versification; ecclesiastical systems; scholastic doctrines. Bah! Give me Walt Whitman and Browning ten times over . . . . The barbarians are in the line of mental growth, and those who do insist that the ideal and the real are dynamically continuous are those by whom the world is to be saved.

William James

Emily Dickinson (1830–1886)

One resents the cavil that makes idiosyncrasy out of individuality, asking why Emily Dickinson should sit in the dim hall to listen to Mrs. Todd's music.

Marianne Moore

William James (1842–1910)

No matter how often what happened had happened any time any one told anything there was no repetition. This is what William James calls the Will to Live. If not nobody would live.

Gertrude Stein

Eventually it [philosophy] landed me squarely in the arms of William James of Harvard, for which God be praised.

W. E. B. Du Bois

Liberty Hyde Bailey (1858–1954)

A vaporous and cryptic prose style obscured the full implications of his "biocentric" message until the 1930s when Aldo Leopold drew directly from Bailey the materials for his own "ecological ethic."

Donald Worster, historian

W. E. B. Du Bois (1868–1963)

My earliest memories of written words . . . those of W. E. B. Du Bois and the Bible.

Langston Hughes

Gertrude Stein (1874–1946)

Again we are reminded that the twentieth century, whatever else it may be, is the century of *Matisse, Picasso and Gertrude Stein*, the title of a Gertrude Stein work whose alternate title, *G.M.P.*, puts Gertrude's initial before the other two, which perhaps is as it should be.

John Ashbery

Charles Ives (1874–1954)

I do know that I don't know how to account for a person who could be indifferent to miracles of dexterity, a certain feat by Don Zimmer—a Dodger at the time—making a backhand catch, of a ball coming hard from behind on the left, fast enough to take his hand off. "The fabric of existence weaves itself whole," as Charles Ives said.

Marianne Moore

Wallace Stevens (1879–1955)

Refusal to speak results here in an eloquence by which we are convinced that America has in Wallace Stevens at least one artist whom professionalism will never demolish.

Marianne Moore

Dear fat Stevens, thawing out so beautifully at forty!

William Carlos Williams

William Carlos Williams (1883–1963)

The pure products of America don't always go crazy. Dr. Williams himself is a demonstration of this.

John Ashbery

Aldo Leopold (1887–1948)

We all strive for safety, prosperity, comfort, long life, and dullness. . . . Perhaps this is behind Thoreau's dictum: In wildness is the salvation of the world.

Aldo Leopold

Robinson Jeffers (1887–1962)

All the mud of mankind's earth-rooted feet, and the sea-wind and sky-wind in men's hair, and their hands that would find a star, and the shock of rock here and star there . . . these things come to rest in Jeffers.

Langston Hughes

13

Marianne Moore (1887–1972)

When you think of what her life might be and what it is—
the way she talks, the things she does, you feel as if you
and she were a pair of sailors just off the boat, determined
to see things through. She is a moral force "in light blue"
at a time when moral forces of any kind are few and far
between.

Wallace Stevens

I consider her the most famous Negro woman poet in
America.

Langston Hughes

Langston Hughes (1902–1967)

Inimitable, irresistible Langston, I do not know why you
were not spoiled with love and care, from the cradle, on,
and were not a proud boy!

Marianne Moore

Lorine Niedecker (1903–1970)

I'd known her about two years, and finally I did sense she
was quite important. I said, "Lorine, who are you?" And she
came right back, not in any boastful way, she said, "William
Carlos Williams said I am the Emily Dickinson of my time."
After that I tried harder.

Gail Roub, her neighbor

Rachel Carson (1907–1964)

I would work most of each night and sleep in the mornings.
There was usually a volume of Thoreau's Journal or of
Richard Jeffries' nature essays beside my bed, and I would
relax my mind by reading a few pages before turning out
the light.

Rachel Carson

Fairfield Porter (1907–1975)

He painted his surroundings as they looked, and they happened to look cozy. But the coziness is deceiving. It reverberates in time the way the fumbled parlor piano tunes in the "Alcotts" section of Ives' *Concord* sonata do.

John Ashbery

James Schuyler (1923–1991)

Sometimes I hear him typing, and often I hear a woodpecker and think it is he. He loves to canoe, and has been in the water, swimming slowly around for a time with a smile on his face, and remarking very gently after a bit, "Why Fairfield. It's the coldest thing I ever felt."

Fairfield Porter

John Ashbery (1927–)

Q: Do you see any new trends in poetry?
A: I wish I did, but I don't. John Ashbery, of course, is a total innovator. He's as innovative as Gertrude Stein.

James Schuyler

Also Appearing

John Winthrop (1588–1649)

For England's sake they are going from England, to pray without ceasing for England!

Edward Johnson

John Cotton (1588–1652)

Mr. Cotton pronounced the sentence of admonition with great solemnity, and with much zeal and detestation of her [Anne Hutchinson's] errors and pride of spirit.

John Winthrop

Decoration Day

I noticed that Robert Browning had made another poem, and was astonished—till I remembered that I, myself, in my smaller way, sang off charnel steps. Every day life feels mightier, and what we have the power to be, more stupendous.

Emily Dickinson

Dedication

I write for myself and strangers, I do this for my own sake and for the sake of those who know I know it that they look like other ones, that they are separate and yet always repeated.

Gertrude Stein

Happy is he who looks only into his work to know if it will succeed, never into the times or the public opinion; and who writes from the love of imparting certain thoughts & not from the necessity of sale—who writes always to *the unknown friend*.

Ralph Waldo Emerson

Democratic Vistas

The end of all good government is to cultivate humanity and promote the happiness of all, and the good of every man in all his rights, his life, liberty, estate, honor, etc., without injury or abuse done to any. . . . And it is as plain as daylight, there is no species of government like a democracy to attain this end. There is but about two steps from an aristocracy to a monarchy, and from thence but one to a tyranny.

John Wise

Man's external, personal, natural liberty, antecedent to all human parts or alliances, must also be considered. And so every man must be conceived to be perfectly in his own power and disposal, and not to be controlled by the authority of any other. And thus every man must be acknowledged equal to every man, since all subjection and all command are equally banished on both sides; and considering all men thus at liberty, every man has a prerogative to judge for himself, *viz.* what shall be most for his behoof, happiness and well-being.

John Wise

The important thing ... is that you must have deep down as the deepest thing in you a sense of equality.

Gertrude Stein

The Discovery of America

Linnaeus said long ago, "Nescio quae facies *laeta, glabra* plantis Americanis" (I know not what there is of joyous and smooth in the aspect of American plants); ... Perchance there will appear to the traveler, he knows not what, of *laeta* and *glabra*, of joyous and serene, in our very faces. Else to what end does the world go on, and why was America discovered?

Henry David Thoreau

One turns with something like ferocity toward a land that one loves, to which one is really and essentially native, to demand that it surrender, reveal, that in itself which one loves. This is a vital affair, not an affair of the heart (as it may be in one's first poems), but an affair of the whole being (as in one's last poems), a fundamental affair of life, or, rather, an affair of fundamental life; so that one's cry of O Jerusalem becomes little by little a cry to something a little nearer and nearer until at last one cries out to a living name, a living place, a living thing, and in crying out confesses openly all the bitter secretions of experience. This is why trivial things often touch us intensely. It is why the sight of an old berry patch, a new growth in the woods in the spring, the particular things on display at a farmers' market, as, for example, the trays of poor apples, the few boxes of black-eyed peas, the bags of dried corn, have an emotional power over us that for a moment is more than we can control.

Wallace Stevens

I have become a vegetable, a suffering vegetable if there be such a thing; and, as like seeks like, I shan't get seriously better until I can get my back onto some American vegetation with an American tree over my head and an American squirrel chittering at me.

William James

Doing Your Thing

Our forefathers walked in the world & went to their graves tormented with the fear of sin & the terror of the Day of Judgment. We are happily rid of those terrors, and our torment is the utter uncertainty & perplexity of what we ought to do; the distrust of the value of what we do; and the distrust that the Necessity which we all at last believe in, is Fair.

Ralph Waldo Emerson

It is awfully important to know what is and what is not your business. I know that one of the most profoundly exciting moments of my life was when at sixteen I suddenly concluded that I would not make all knowledge my province.

Gertrude Stein

Life is a selection, no more. The work of the gardener is simply to destroy this weed, or that shrub, or that tree, & leave this other to grow. The library is gradually made inestimable by taking out from the superabounding mass of books all but the best. The palace is a selection of materials; its architecture, a selection of the best effects. Things collect very fast of themselves; the difference between house & house is the wise omissions.

Ralph Waldo Emerson

After the early period of absorbing influences from the art and other things going on around one comes a period of consolidation when one locks the door in order to sort out what one has and to make of it what one can. It's not a question—at least I hope it isn't—of shutting oneself off from further influences: these do arrive, and sometimes, although rarely, can outweigh the earlier ones. It's rather a question of conserving and using what one has acquired.

John Ashbery

Do your thing & I shall know you.*

Ralph Waldo Emerson

Droll Yankee

Am I the American indeed—I can't be entirely content, it
seems, without some puzzlement, some sharpness, a bit of
word-play, a kind of rhythm and music in however small a
way. . . .

Lorine Niedecker

---

*Lost in Translation

Some of the young people in college today probably don't believe
this, but people used to talk like those movies of the 60s. They
thought drug use was "cool" and advised you to "Do your own
thing." Well, if somebody said that to you today, you'd probably think
they got lost in a time-warp during one of the original runs of "Star
Trek."
—George Bush, October 7, 1988

I've gotten over being offended by the columns that misconstrue
who I am. I do my thing, and they do theirs.
—George Bush, October 12, 1988

Do your own thing. Don't be afraid to give your opinion. Just be-
cause you're married doesn't mean you've given up your right to
have an opinion.
—Nancy Reagan, January 15, 1989

The doctrine of do your own thing, you do your thing and I will do
mine, led to drug abuse in America.
—William J. Bennett, December 1, 1989

You always get ups and downs. We're going to just do our thing, and
we'll be fine.
—Barbara Bush, November 12, 1990

Some things can be done as well as others.
—Sam Patch, October 29, 1829

I saw two Bushes fight just now—The wind was to blame—
but to see them differ was pretty as a Lawsuit

Emily Dickinson

Dying Words

Moose. Indian.

Henry David Thoreau

Each and All

I need hardly say to any one acquainted with my thoughts
that I have no system. When I was quite young I fancied
that by keeping a Manuscript Journal by me, over whose
pages I wrote a great list of the topics of human study, as,
Religion, Poetry, Politics, Love, &c in the course of a few years
I should be able to complete a sort of Encyclopaedia contain-
ing the net value of all the definitions at which the world
had yet arrived. But at the end of a couple of years my
Cabinet Cyclopaedia though much enlarged was no nearer
to a completeness than on its first day. Nay somehow the
whole plan of it needed alteration nor did the following
months promise any speedier term to it than the foregoing.
At last I discovered that my curve was a parabola whose arcs
would never meet, and came to acquiesce in the perception
that although no diligence can rebuild the Universe in a
model by the best accumulation or disposition of details, yet
does the World reproduce itself in miniature in every event
that transpires, so that all the laws of nature may be read in
the smallest fact. So that the truth speaker may dismiss all
solicitude as to the proportion & congruency of the aggre-
gate of his thoughts so long as he is a faithful reporter of
particular impressions.

Ralph Waldo Emerson

Economy

I am glad you love the Blossoms so well.
I hope you love Birds too.

It is economical. It saves going to Heaven.

Emily Dickinson

Effects of Analogy

There is something endearing about a young spruce cone,
one that is just ripening, like a baby tortoise.

James Schuyler

The other day at last I saw as well as heard a whitethroat
sparrow. He, or she, or it, was quite near and the giant sound
seemed all around it, and it took a moment to be sure that
little fluffy ball was its source. A little like the exquisite thread
of sound that came out of short, vast Lina Paliughi. More like
the short skinny boy in the barrack at Key West with the
enormous cock behind which he would come from the shower
with an air of disclaimer and acceptance. The hooting and
teasing he got was not without good-natured pride: after all, it
lived in *our* barrack. And overhead, day and night, the big
fans revolved.

James Schuyler

Empowerment

It would be a pity to dissolve the union & so diminish im-
mensely every man's personal importance.

Ralph Waldo Emerson

The End of Beauty

It will probably be centuries, at least generations, before man
will discover all or even most of the value in a quarter-tone
extension. And when he does, nature has plenty of other

things up her sleeve. And it may be longer than we think before the ear will freely translate what it hears and instinctively arouse and amplify the spiritual consciousness.

But that needn't keep anyone from trying to find out how to use a few more of the myriads of sound waves nature has put around in the air (immune from the radio) for man to catch if he can and "perchance make himself a part with nature," as Thoreau used to say.

Charles Ives

There are beauties that are more palpable and explicable, and there are hidden and secret beauties. The former pleases, and we can tell why; we can explain the particular point for the agreement that renders the thing pleasing. Such are all artificial regularities; we can tell wherein the regularity lies that affects us. [The] latter sort are those beauties that delight us and we cannot tell why. . . . These hidden beauties are commonly by far the greatest, because the more complex a beauty is, the more hidden is it.

Jonathan Edwards

I think ten million supple-wristed gods are always hiding beauty in the world—burying it every where in every thing—and most of all in spots that men and women do not think of and never look—as Death and Poverty and Wickedness.—Cache! and Cache again! all over the earth, and in the heavens that swathe the earth, and in the waters of the sea.—They do their jobs well; those journeymen divine. Only from the Poet they can hide nothing and would not if they could.—I reckon he is Boss of those gods; and the work they do is done for him; and all they have concealed, they have concealed for his sake.—Him they attend indoors and outdoors.—They run ahead when he walks, and lift their cunning covers and signify him with pointed stretched arms.

Walt Whitman

The processes of art, to keep alive, must always challenge the unknown and go where the most uncertainty lies. So that beauty when it is found, as it rarely is, shall have a touch of the marvelous about it, the unknown. If it were not so, it would be the end of beauty.

William Carlos Williams

The End of History

To the Twentieth Century events are not important. You must know that. Events are not exciting. Events have lost their interest for people. You read them more like a soothing syrup, and if you listen over the radio you don't get very excited. The thing has got to this place, that events are so wonderful that they are not exciting. Now you have to remember that the business of an artist is to be exciting.

Gertrude Stein

This as I say has been the great problem of our generation, so much happens and anybody at any moment knows everything that is happening that things happening although interesting are not really exciting. And an artist an artist inevitably has to do what is really exciting. That is what he is inside him, that is what an artist really is inside him, he is exciting, and if he is not there is nothing to any of it.

Gertrude Stein

On the other hand, perhaps these are the most exciting times for young artists, who must fight even harder to preserve their identity. Before they were fighting against general neglect, even hostility, but this seemed like a natural thing and therefore the fight could be carried on in good faith. Today one must fight acceptance which is much harder because it seems that one is fighting oneself.

John Ashbery

End of Ideology

What are philosophers, scientists, religionists, they that have filled up literature with their pap? Writers, of a kind. Stein simply erases their stories, turns them off and does without them, their logic (founded merely on the limits of the perceptions) which is supposed to transcend the words, along with them. Stein denies it. The words, in writing, she discloses, transcend everything.

William Carlos Williams

Epigraph

Perchance, when, in the course of ages, American liberty has become a fiction of the past,—as it is to some extent a fiction of the present,—the poets of the world will be inspired by American mythology.

Henry David Thoreau

E Pluribus Unum

We Americans have yet to really learn our own antecedents, and sort them, to unify them. They will be found ampler than supposed, and in widely different sources. . . . Character, literature, a society worthy of the name, are yet to be establish'd, through a nationality of noblest spiritual, heroic and democratic attributes—not one of which at present definitely exists—entirely different from the past, though unerringly founded on it, and to justify it.

Walt Whitman

Manistique, Indian name for vermillion (the colored earth the Indians used—or worm, actually?—to paint their faces). We stayed overnight here. Mfg. city and resort.

  Al: The natives pronounce it MAN´ isty.

  I: So be it. The North is one vast, massive glorious corruption of rock and language—granite is underlaid with limestone or sandstone, gneiss is made-over granite, shale, or sandstone and so forth and so on and Thompsonite (or Thomsonite) is often mistaken for agate and agate is shipped in from Mexico and Uruguay and can even be artificially dyed in the bargain. And look what's been done to language!— People of all nationalities and color have changed the language like weather and pressure have changed the rocks.

Lorine Niedecker

As to that composite American identity of the future, Spanish character will supply some of the most needed parts. . . . Who knows but that element, like the course of some subterranean river, dipping invisibly for a hundred or two years, is now to emerge in broadest flow and permanent action?

Walt Whitman

Equal Protection

And in this country one sees that there is always margin enough in the statute for a liberal judge to read one way and a servile judge another.

Ralph Waldo Emerson

Errand into the Wilderness

There is another combination of virtues strangely mixed in every lively, holy Christian: and that is, diligence in worldly businesses, and yet deadness to the world. Such a mystery as none can read but they that know it.

John Cotton

The "ability to be drunk with a sudden realization of value in things others never notice" can metamorphose our detestable reasonableness and offset a whole planetary system of deadness.

Marianne Moore

Talk of mysteries! Think of our life in nature—daily to be shown matter, to come in contact with it,—rocks, trees, wind on our cheeks! the *solid* earth! the *actual* world! the *common sense! Contact! Contact! Who* are we? *where* are we?

Henry David Thoreau

Now, here lies a difficulty and here is a reason for writing this book: the population of the earth is increasing, the relative population of farmers is decreasing, people are herding in cities, we have a city mind, and relatively fewer people are brought in touch with the earth in any real way. So it is incumbent on us to take special pains—now that we see the new time—that all the people, or as many of them as possible, shall have contact with the earth and that the earth righteousness shall be abundantly taught.

Liberty Hyde Bailey

He will have the earth receive and return his affection; he will stay with it as the bridegroom stays with the bride. The cool-breath'd ground, the slumbering and liquid trees, the just-gone sunset, the vitreous pour of the full moon, the tender and growing night, he salutes and touches, and they touch him. The sea supports him, and hurries him off with its powerful and crooked fingers. Dash me with amorous wet! then, he says; I can repay you.

Walt Whitman

Oh Matchless Earth—We underrate the chance to dwell in Thee

Emily Dickinson

Expanding Universe

I live a good while & acquire as much skill in literature as an old carpenter does in wood. It occurs, then, what pity, that now, when you know something, have at least learned so much good omission, your organs should fail you; your eyes, health, fire & zeal of work, should decay daily. Then I remember that it is the mind of the world which is the good carpenter, the good scholar, sailor, or blacksmith, thousand-handed, versatile, all-applicable. . . . In you, this rich soul has peeped, despite your horny muddy eyes, at books & poetry. Well, it took you up, & showed you something to the purpose; that there was something there. Look, look, old mole! there, straight up before you, is the magnificent Sun. If only for the instant, you see it. Well, in this way it educates the youth of the Universe; in this way, warms, suns, refines every particle; then it drops the little channel or canal, through which the Life rolled beatific—like a fossil to the ground—thus touched & educated by a moment of sunshine, to be the fairer material for future channels & canals, through which the old Glory shall dart again, in new directions, until the Universe shall have been shot through & through, *tilled* with light.

Ralph Waldo Emerson

Fame

Do you see what I mean when I say anybody in America can be a public one, and anybody in America being able to be a public one it has something to do with the hero crime and so many people are always doing this thing doing the hero crime it gets into anybody who can have his picture where it is to be seen by everybody. Of course there are so many who feel themselves to be a crime hero that practically nobody wonders that there are any, their names are like the names of Pullman cars, they make them up as easily and it is no good.

Gertrude Stein

Fashion

Whatever the cut, width, or foot, the wearer should be able to step with assurance—as Dante says, like a crane—"come una crana."

Marianne Moore

Fate of the Earth

Life is a spell so exquisite that everything conspires to break it.

Emily Dickinson

Some of the thoughts that came were so unattractive to me that I rejected them completely, for the old ideas die hard, especially when they are emotionally as well as intellectually dear to one. It was pleasant to believe, for example, that much of Nature was forever beyond the tampering reach of man: he might level the forests and dam the streams, but the clouds and the rain and the wind were God's . . . . It was comforting to suppose that the stream of life would flow on through time in whatever course that God had appointed for it—without interference by one of the drops of the stream, man. And to suppose that, however the physical environment might mold Life, that Life could never assume the power to change drastically—or even destroy—the physical world.

These beliefs have almost been part of me for as long as I have thought about such things. To have them even vaguely threatened was so shocking that, as I have said, I shut my mind—refused to acknowledge what I couldn't help seeing. But that does no good, and I have now opened my eyes and my mind. I may not like what I see, but it does no good to ignore it, and it's worse than useless to go repeating the old "eternal verities" that are no more eternal than the hills of the poets. So it seems time someone wrote of Life in the light of the truth as it now appears to us.

Rachel Carson

Torrential rains, water rising at Fort, my husband's cucumbers & squash swimming. Depend on nothing.

Lorine Niedecker

Foreign Affairs

I was much taken with what one American soldier said when he was in England. He said we did not get along at all with the

English until they finally did get it in their heads that we were not cousins, but foreigners, once they really got that, there was no more trouble.

Gertrude Stein

And for Americans who feel that America is the last truly foreign country. . . .

John Ashbery

Form Follows Function

Let a brave, devout man spend the year in the woods of Maine or Labrador, and see if the Hebrew Scriptures speak adequately to his condition and experience, from the setting in of winter to the breaking up of the ice.

Henry David Thoreau

You spoke of "Hope" surpassing "Home"—I thought that Hope *was* Home—a misapprehension of Architecture—but then if I knew . . .

Emily Dickinson

Even as a boy, I had the fancy, the wish, to write a piece, perhaps a poem, about the sea-shore—that suggesting, dividing line, contact, junction, the solid marrying with the liquid—that curious, lurking something, (as doubtless every objective form finally becomes to the subjective spirit,) which means far more than its mere first sight, grand as that is—blending the real and ideal, and each made portion of the other. Hours, days, in my Long Island youth and early manhood, I haunted the shores of Rockaway or Coney island, or away east to the Hamptons or Montauk. Once, at the latter place, (by the old lighthouse, nothing but sea-tossings in sight in every direction as far as the eye could reach,) I remember well, I felt that I must one day write a book expressing this liquid, mystic theme. Afterward, I recollect, how it came to me that instead of any special lyrical or epical or literary attempt, the sea-shore should be an invisible *influ-*

ence, a pervading gauge and tally for me, in my composition. (Let me give a hint here to young writers. I am not sure but I have unwittingly follow'd out the same rule with other powers beside sea and shores—avoiding them, in the way of any dead set at poetizing them, as too big for formal handling— quite satisfied if I could indirectly show that we have met and fus'd, even if only once, but enough—that we have really absorb'd each other and understand each other.)

There is a dream, a picture, that for years at intervals, (sometimes quite long ones, but surely again, in time,) has come noiselessly up before me, and I really believe, fiction as it is, has enter'd largely into my practical life—certainly into my writings, and shaped and color'd them. It is nothing more or less than a stretch of interminable white-brown sand, hard and smooth and broad, with the ocean perpetually, grandly, rolling in upon it, with slow-measured sweep, with rustle and hiss and foam, and many a thump as of low bass drums. This scene, this picture, I say, has risen before me at times for years. Sometimes I wake at night and can hear and see it plainly.

Walt Whitman

Founding Fathers

We, John Wise, John Andrews, sen., Robert Kinsman, Wm. Goodhue, jr., all of Ipswich, about 22d of Aug., 1687, were, with several principal inhabitants of Ipswich, met at Mr. John Appleton's, and there discoursed and concluded, that it was not the town's duty any way to assist that ill method of raising money without a General Assembly, which was apparently intended by abovesaid Sir Edmund and his Council, as witness a late act issued out by them for such a purpose. The next day in a general town-meeting of the inhabitants of Ipswich, we, the abovenamed J. Wise, J. Andrews, R. Kinsman, W. Goodhue, with the rest of the town, there met, (none contradicting,) and gave our assent to the vote then made.... We, the complainants, with Mr. John Appleton and Thomas French, all of Ipswich, were brought to answer for the said vote out of our own county, thirty or forty miles into Suffolk and in Boston, kept in jail for contempt and high misdemeanor, as our mittimus specifies, and, upon demand, denied the privilege of Habeas Corpus, and from prison overruled to answer at a Court of Oyer and Terminer in Boston. . . . In our defence was pleaded the repeal of the Law of Assessment upon the place; also the Magna Charta of England, and the Statute Laws, that secure the subjects' properties and estates, &c. To which was replied by one of the judges, the rest by silence assenting, that we must not think the laws of England follow us to the ends of the earth, or whither we went. And the same person (J. Wise abovesaid testifies) declared in open council, upon examination of said Wise, "Mr. Wise, you have no more privileges left you, than not to be sold as slaves," and no man in Council contradicted. By such laws our trial and trouble began and ended. Mr. Dudley, aforesaid Chief Judge, to close up the debate and trial, trims up a speech that pleased himself (as we suppose) more than the people. Among many other remarkable passages to this purpose, he bespeaks the jury's obedience, who (we suppose) were very well pre-inclined, viz. "I am glad," says he, "there be so many worthy gentlemen of the jury so capable to do the King's service, and we expect a good verdict from you, seeing the matter hath been so sufficiently proved against the criminals."

John Wise

I have faced during my life many unpleasant experiences: the growl of a mob; the personal threat of murder; the scowling distaste of an audience. But nothing has cowed me as that day, November 8, 1951, when I took my seat in a Washington courtroom as an indicted criminal.

W. E. B. Du Bois

Free Enterprise

I found you were gone, by accident, as I find Systems are, or Seasons of the year, and obtain no cause—but suppose it a treason of Progress—that dissolves as it goes—

Emily Dickinson

Americans don't own their high standard of living, they only rent it, which means that they are likely to lose it suddenly as so many did in the Depression.

Gertrude Stein

We peddle, we truck, we sail, we row, we ride in cars, we creep in teams, we go in canals,—to market, and for the sale of goods. The national aim and employment streams into our ways of thinking, our laws, our habits and our manners. The customer is the immediate jewel of our souls. Him we flatter, him we feast, compliment, vote for, and will not contradict. It was, or it seemed the dictate of trade, to keep the negro down. We had found a race who were less warlike, and less energetic shopkeepers than we; who had very little skill in trade. We found it very convenient to keep them at work, since by the aid of a little whipping, we could get their work for nothing but their board and the cost of the whips. What if it cost a few unpleasant scenes on the coast of Africa? . . . The sugar they raised was excellent: nobody tasted blood in it. The coffee was fragrant; the tobacco was incense; the brandy made nations happy; the cotton clothed the world. What! all raised by these men, and no wages! Excellent! What a convenience!

Ralph Waldo Emerson

When the ordinary American hears of cases of injustice he begins to pooh-pooh and minimize and tone down the thing, and breed excuses from his general fund of optimism and respect for expediency. "It's understandable from the point of view of the parties interested"—but understandable in onlooking citizens only as a symptom of the moral flabbiness born of the exclusive worship of the bitch-goddess SUCCESS. That—with the squalid cash interpretation put on the word success—is our national disease.

William James

The real wealth of the Nation lies in the resources of the earth—soil, water, forests, minerals, and wildlife. . . . For many years public-spirited citizens throughout the country have been working for the conservation of the natural resources, realizing their vital importance to the Nation. Apparently their hard-won progress is to be wiped out, as a politically minded Administration returns us to the dark ages of unrestrained exploitation and destruction.

Rachel Carson

Strange it is, however, that we should not have insisted at least that those who appropriate the accumulations of the earth should complete their work, cleaning up the remainders, leaving the areas wholesome, inoffensive and safe. How many and many are the years required to grow a forest and to fill the pockets of the rocks, and how satisfying are the landscapes, and yet how desperately soon men may reduce it all to ruin and to emptiness, and how slatternly may they violate the scenery!

Liberty Hyde Bailey

This afternoon, being on Fair Haven Hill, I heard the sound of a saw, and soon after from the Cliff saw two men sawing down a noble pine beneath, about forty rods off. I resolved to watch it till it fell, the last of a dozen or more which were left when the forest was cut and for fifteen years have waved in solitary majesty over the sproutland. I have seen them like beavers or insects gnawing at the trunk of this noble tree, the diminutive manikins with their crosscut saw which could scarcely span it. It towered up a hundred feet as I afterward found by measurement, one of the tallest probably in the township and straight as an arrow, but slanting a little toward the hillside, its top seen against the frozen river and the hills of Conantum. I watch closely to see when it begins to move. Now the sawyers stop, and with an axe open it a little on the side toward which it leans, that it may break the faster. And now their saw goes again. Now surely it is going; it is inclined one quarter of the quadrant, and, breathless, I expect its crashing fall. But, no, I was mistaken; it has not moved an inch; it stands at the same angle as at first. It is fifteen minutes yet to its fall. Still its branches wave in the wind, as if it were destined to stand for a century, and the wind soughs through its needles as of yore; it is still a forest tree, the most

33

majestic tree that waves over Musketaquid. The silvery sheen of the sunlight is reflected from its needles; it still affords an inaccessible crotch for the squirrel's nest; not a lichen has forsaken its mast-like stem, its raking mast—the hill is the hulk. Now, now's the moment! The manikins at its base are fleeing from their crime. They have dropped the guilty saw and the axe. How slowly and majestically it starts! as if it were only swayed by a summer breeze, and would return without a sigh to its location in the air. And now it fans the hillside with its fall, and it lies down to its bed in the valley, from which it is never to rise, as softly as a feather, folding its green mantle about it like a warrior, as if, tired of standing, it embraced the earth with silent joy, returning its elements to the dust again. But hark! there you only saw, but did not hear. There now comes up a deafening crash to these rocks, advertising you that even trees do not die without a groan. It rushes to embrace the earth, and mingle its elements with the dust. And now all is still once more and forever, both to eye and ear.

Henry David Thoreau

Since we have written you, the grand Rail Road decision is made, and there is great rejoicing throughout this town and the neighboring; that is Sunderland, Montague, and Belchertown. Every body is wide awake, every thing is stirring, the streets are full of people talking cheeringly, and you really should be here to partake of the jubilee. The event was celebrated by D. Warner, and cannon; and the silent satisfaction in the hearts of all is it's crowning attestation.

Father is really *sober* from excessive satisfaction, and bears his honors with a most becoming air. Nobody *believes* it yet, it seems like a fairy tale, a most *miraculous* event in the lives of us all. The men begin working next week, only think of it, Austin; why I verily believe we shall fall down and worship the first "Son of Erin" that comes, and the first sod he turns will be preserved as an emblem of the struggles and victory of our heroic fathers.

Emily Dickinson

Free Speech

Those things most listened for, certainly those are the things least said.

Walt Whitman

The Unbelief of the age is attested by the loud condemnation of trifles. Look at our silly religious papers. Let a minister wear a cane, or a white hat, go to a theatre, or avoid a sunday school, let a school book with a Calvinistic sentence or a sunday schoolbook without one, be heard of, & instantly all the old grannies squeak & gibber & do what they call sounding an alarm, from Bangor to Mobile. Alike nice & squeamish is its ear; you must on no account say "stink" or "damn."

Ralph Waldo Emerson

Personally, I DO NOT LIKE RADIO, and I feel that it is almost as far from being a free medium of expression for Negro writers as Hitler's airplanes are for the Jews.

Langston Hughes

Although mid-twentieth century of the middle ages continued had brought me the printing press, I'd found that Wm. James was right: "The sensational press is the organ of a state of mind which means a new 'dark' ages that may last more centuries than the first one. Then illiteracy was brutal and dumb and power was rapacious without disguise. Now illiteracy has an enormous literary organization and power is sophistical;" and this organization, as good an avenue for plunder as any business is, protects and is protected by that other and still more expensive organization, war. I'd found that a job does not necessarily sustain life.

Lorine Niedecker

There is much in life and there is much in art that is not productive of complaisance. One enjoys a sense of magnanimity in George Washington's dismounting to assist a stranger to right an overturned carriage, and denies implication in the slave auction—in the "sickly" creature's going for little and the "good" one's selling for more; but both incidents are really ourselves and are in the eyes of honesty, to be verified.

Marianne Moore

Free Trade

A man coquetting with too many countries is as bad as a bigamist, and loses his soul altogether.

William James

The Future

All we know is that it will change, and in art, in a sense, all change has to be for the better, since it shows that the artist hasn't yet given in to the ever-present temptation to stand still and that his constantly menaced vitality is emitting signals.

John Ashbery

Generation Gap

I would have been hailed with approval if I had died at 50. At 75 my death was practically requested. If living does not give value, wisdom and meaning to life, then there is no sense in living at all. If immature and inexperienced men rule the earth, then the earth deserves what it gets: the repetition of age-old mistakes, and wild welcome for what men knew a thousand years ago was disaster.

W. E. B. Du Bois

"The Classics," "the Classics"! forsooth; as if there were only twenty or thirty books to set the pitch for all thought, and as if every man was not a new world and his thinking new, entire, and perfect. Ah me! Is there any tragedy so dire as this deliquium, of this falling back, this epilepsy, this old age? that virtue should pause; and intellect pause, and decease out of the body, *it* remaining to drivel on for the pleasure of the senses. See that all that has been done in the planet was done by young men.

Ralph Waldo Emerson

Age and youth are great flatterers. Brooding on each other's obvious psychology neither dares tell the other outright what manifestly is the truth: your world is poison.

William Carlos Williams

We do not think enough of the Dead as exhilirants—they are not dissuaders but Lures—Keepers of that great Romance still to us foreclosed—while coveting (we envy) their wisdom we lament their silence . . . That they have existed none can take away. That they still exist is a trust so daring we thank thee that thou hast hid these things from us and hast revealed them to them. The power and the glory are the post mortuary gifts.

Emily Dickinson

Our understanding of human relations has grown—more perhaps than we realize in the last twenty years; and when Henry James disappoints us by retaining the Northerner's feeling about the Confederate, we must not make him directly contemporary, any more than we dispute his spelling "peanut" with a hyphen.

Marianne Moore

And so I do know what a genius is, a genius is some one who does not have to remember the two hundred years that everybody else has to remember.

Gertrude Stein

The Geographical History of America

Massachusetts
John Wise, b. Roxbury
Ralph Waldo Emerson, b. Boston
Margaret Fuller, b. Cambridgeport
Henry David Thoreau, b. Concord
Emily Dickinson, b. Amherst
W. E. B. Du Bois, b. Great Barrington

Connecticut
Jonathan Edwards, b. East Windsor
Charles Ives, b. Danbury

New York
Walt Whitman, b. West Hills
William James, b. New York
John Ashbery, b. Rochester

Michigan
Liberty Hyde Bailey, b. South Haven

Pennsylvania
Gertrude Stein, b. Allegheny
Wallace Stevens, b. Reading
Robinson Jeffers, b. Allegheny
Rachel Carson, b. Springdale

New Jersey
William Carlos Williams, b. Rutherford

Iowa
Aldo Leopold, b. Burlington

Missouri
Marianne Moore, b. Kirkwood
Langston Hughes, b. Joplin

Wisconsin
Lorine Niedecker, b. Fort Atkinson

Illinois
Fairfield Porter, b. Winnetka
James Schuyler, b. Chicago

Global Village

And in proportion as a man has bestirred himself to become awake to his own locality he will perceive more and more of what is disclosed and find himself in a position to make the necessary translations. The disclosures will then and only then come to him as reality, as joy, as release. For these men communicate with each other and strive to invent new devices. But he who does not know his own world, in whatever confused form it may be, must either stupidly fail to learn from foreign work or stupidly swallow it without knowing how to judge of its essential value. Descending each his own branch man and man reach finally a common trunk of understanding.

William Carlos Williams

Golden Rule

For I suppose that liberty is an accurate index, in men and nations, of general progress. The theory of personal liberty must always appeal to the most refined communities . . . . For it is,—is it not?,—the essence of courtesy, of politeness, of religion, of love, to prefer another, to postpone oneself, to protect another from oneself?

Ralph Waldo Emerson

Habits of the Heart

The manners of young men who are still engaged heart &
soul in uttering their Protest against society as they find it, are
perchance disagreeable; their whole being seems rough &
unmelodious; but have a little patience. And do not exagger-
ate the offence of that particular objection which with such
undue and absurd dogmatism they make every day from
morn till dewy eve. The institutions of society come across
each ingenuous & original soul in some different point. One
feels the jar in Marriage; one in Property; one in Money; one
in Church; one in social Conventions; one in Slavery; one in
War; each feels it in some one & a different point according to
his own circumstance & history & for a long time does not see
that it is a central falsehood which he is contending against, &
that his protest against a particular superficial falsehood will
surely ripen with time & insight into a deeper & Universal
grudge.

Ralph Waldo Emerson

Of Miss P—I know but this, dear. She wrote me in October,
requesting me to aid the world by my chirrup more. Perhaps
she stated it as my duty, I don't distinctly remember, and
always burn such letters so I cannot obtain it now. I replied
declining. She did not write to me again—she might have
been offended, or perhaps is extricating humanity from some
hopeless ditch.

Emily Dickinson

Hidden Agenda

What umpire can there be between us but the future? In
other words, we are all fated to be *a priori* teleologists, whether
we will or not. Interests which we bring with us, and simply
posit or take our stand upon, are the very flour out of which
our mental dough is kneaded. The optimism of thought,
from the vague dawn of discomfort or ease in the polyp to the
intellectual joy of Laplace among his formulas, is teleological

through and through. Not a cognition occurs but feeling is there to comment on it, to stamp it as of greater or less worth.

William James

The beginnings are slow and infirm, but it is an always-accelerated march. The geologic world is chronicled by the growing ripeness of the strata from lower to higher, as it becomes the abode of more highly organized plants and animals. The civil history of men might be traced by the successive meliorations as marked in higher moral generalizations;— virtue meaning physical courage, then chastity and temperance, then justice and love;—bargains of kings with peoples of certain rights to certain classes, then of rights to masses,—then at last came the day when, as the historians rightly tell, the nerves of the world were electrified by the proclamation that all men are born free and equal.

Ralph Waldo Emerson

Higher Education

If it were possible for every person to own a tree and to care for it, the good results would be beyond estimation.

Liberty Hyde Bailey

High Tech

What a Hazard a Letter is!
When I think of the Hearts it has scuttled and sunk, I almost fear to lift my Hand to so much as a Superscription.

Emily Dickinson

History

Let us start at the bottom. We are constantly aware of what might have been. It is quite a different thing from having a sense of the past. We have imagined things that we have failed to realize. Now, go back to the beginning. Our imagination of or concerning the world so completely transformed it that, looking back at it, it was a true land's end, a relic of farewells. But this transformation having been effected, the imagination with its typical nostalgia for reality tried to go back to recover the world. It was not so much a remote land's end as something that changed its identity, denied its familiar intelligence (fought against its thoughts and dreams, as if these were an alphabet with which it could not spell out its riddle). With every transformation, with the fluctuations between reality and imagination and the inescapable and frequent returns to reality, a mountainous music always seemed to be passing away.

Wallace Stevens

Only Nature has a right to grieve perpetually, for she only is innocent.

Henry David Thoreau

Home

It hath been always observed here, that such as fell into discontent, and lingered after their former conditions in England, fell into the scurvy and died.

John Winthrop

After all anybody is as their land and air is. Anybody is as the sky is low or high, the air heavy or clear and anybody is as there is wind or no wind there. It is that which makes them and the arts they make and the work they do and the way they eat and the way they drink and the way they learn and everything.

Gertrude Stein

Had I not heard as a child in the little churches of Kansas and Missouri, "Deep river, my home is over Jordan," or "My Lord, what a morning when the stars begin to fall," I might not have come to realize the lyric beauty of *living* poetry. . . . Could you possibly be afraid that the rest of the world will not accept it?

Our spirituals are sung and loved in the great concert halls of the whole world. Our blues are played from Topeka to Tokyo. Harlem's jive talk delights Hong Kong and Paris. Those of our writers who have *most* concerned themselves with our very special problems are translated and read around the world. The local, the regional can—and does—become universal. Sean O'Casey's Irishmen are an example. So I would say to young Negro writers, do not be afraid of yourself. *You* are the world.

Langston Hughes

They say that "home is where the heart is." I think it is where the *house* is, and the adjacent buildings.

Emily Dickinson

There is a commonplace beauty about "Orchard House"—a kind of spiritual sturdiness underlying its quaint picturesqueness—a kind of common triad of the New England homestead, whose overtones tell us that there must have been something aesthetic fibered in the Puritan severity— the self-sacrificing part of the ideal—a value that seems to stir a deeper feeling, a stronger sense of being nearer some perfect truth than a Gothic cathedral or an Etruscan villa. All around you, under the Concord sky, there still floats the influence of that human-faith-melody—transcendent and sentimental enough for the enthusiast or the cynic, respectively—reflecting an innate hope, a common interest in common things and common men—a tune the Concord bards are ever playing while they pound away at the immensities with a Beethoven-like sublimity, and with, may we say, a vehemence and perseverance, for that part of greatness is not so difficult to emulate.

Charles Ives

Life is an affair of people not of places. But for me life is an affair of places and that is the trouble.

Wallace Stevens

We have as good right, and the same sort of right to be here, as Cape Cod or Sandy Hook have to be there.

Ralph Waldo Emerson

How To Be Your Own Best Friend

Take for granted that you've got a temperament from which you must make up your mind to expect twenty times as much anguish as other people need to get along with. Regard it as something as external to you as possible, like the curl of your hair. Remember when old December's darkness is every where about you, that the world is really in every minutest point as full of life as in the most joyous morning you ever lived through; that the sun is whanging down, and the waves dancing, and the gulls skimming down at the mouth of the Amazon, for instance, as freshly as in the first morning of creation; and the hour is just as fit as any hour that ever was for a new gospel of cheer to be preached. I am sure that one can, by merely thinking of these matters of fact, limit the power of one's evil moods over one's way of looking at the Kosmos.

William James

If you have no faith in beneficent power above you, but see only an adamantine fate coiling its folds about nature and man, then reflect that the best use of fate is to teach us courage, if only because baseness cannot change the appointed event. If you accept your thoughts as inspirations from the Supreme Intelligence, obey them when they prescribe difficult duties, because they come only so long as they are used; or, if your skepticism reaches to the last verge, and you have no confidence in any foreign mind, then be brave, because there is one good opinion which must always be of consequence to you, namely, your own.

Ralph Waldo Emerson

Is not the sweet resentment of friends that we are not strong, more inspiriting even than the strength itself?

Talent, knowledge, humility, reverence, magnanimity involve the inconvenience of responsibility or they die. To the bonanza, the legacy, the professional hit, it would be well if our attitude were that of the Brazilian dazzled by unearthing a *calderião* (cluster of diamonds): "My Lord and Heavenly father, if this wealth endangers my soul, let it vanish." It is what every poem is about, as Robert Frost writes, "the triumph of the spirit over the materialism by which we are being smothered."

Example is needed, not counsel; but let me submit here these four precepts:

Feed imagination food that invigorates.
Whatever it is, do it with all your might.
Never do to another what you would not wish done to
    yourself.
Say to yourself, "I will be responsible."

Put these principles to the test, and you will be inconvenienced by being overtrusted, overbefriended, overconsulted, half adopted, and have no leisure. Face that when you come to it.

Marianne Moore

How Writing Is Written

Tell children what you say about writing & laboring with the hands. I know better. Can you distil rum by minding it at odd times? or analyze soils? or carry on the Suffolk Bank? or the Greenwich Observatory? or sail a ship through the Narrows by minding the helm when you happen to think of it? or serve a glass-house, or a steam-engine, or a telegraph, or a rail-road express? or accomplish anything good or anything powerful in this manner? Nothing whatever. And the greatest of all arts, the subtlest, & of most miraculous effect, you

45

fancy is to be practiced with a pen in one hand & a crowbar or a peat-knife in the other. All power is of geometrical increase.

Ralph Waldo Emerson

The sense of strangeness, may we say, is an illusion. Those with keen perceptions may suffer more than others, but the same sufferings and desperations are common to each and in almost the same way. One goes into a friend's study. The books, prints, convenient desk, make one feel that one could work in such a place. Others have a similar impression of one's own surroundings—that seem to one at times like a subway at the rush hour, or a way-station on a cinder-bank.

Marianne Moore

As at all times I write practically every day and if you write not long but practically every day you do get a great deal written.

Gertrude Stein

The important thing is not to get discouraged if you miss a day, or a week, or even a few months. It's only when you start missing entire years that you should become concerned.

James Schuyler

So far in this world, only my writing has been my own, to do when I wanted to do it, to finish only when I felt it was finished, to put it aside or discard it completely if I chose. . . . I have washed thousands of hotel dishes, cooked, scrubbed decks, worked 12 to 15 hours a day on a farm, swallowed my pride for the help of philanthropy and charity—but nobody ever said to me, "you must write now. You must finish that poem tomorrow. You must begin to create on the first of the month."

Langston Hughes

On days when I want to write I will usually waste the morning and go for an afternoon walk to Greenwich Village. (I live near by in Chelsea, which is a pleasant place to walk from though maybe not to.) Sometimes this takes too long and my preferred late afternoon moment will pass. I can't really work at night. Nor in the morning, very much, when I have more ideas but am less critical of them, it seems. I never can use the time I waste doing this for some other purpose like answering letters. It's no good for anything but wasting.

John Ashbery

The length of his walk uniformly made the length of his writing. If shut up in the house he [Thoreau] did not write at all.

Ralph Waldo Emerson

One of the essential conditions to the writing of poetry is impetus.

Wallace Stevens

Human Nature

Nature, last week, including human nature. I had mowed by hand to the river—half way down the middle of the path I found two red dogwood and the sweetest little ash sapling. I knew I'd have to put a fence around 'em if I ever wanted to keep 'em from harm but I let it go unfenced for a whole day. But in those twenty-four hours my neighbor who has a power mowing machine came over and in his zeal mowed me down my dogwoods and tree. Conservationists out here! Also he destroys all the teal duck nests with his infernal machine. Then the killdeer nest on the pile of stones on the other side of me— the children up the line came and found the eggs lying on the stones (the bird didn't bother to build a nest, just laid the eggs on the rocks), and took 'em home—their mothers made 'em put the eggs back and lo the bird is sitting on 'em as tho nothing ever happened. I've read that birds don't usually want to go back on eggs that have been handled, but this one is different, it seems. Of course, she may soon find out whether or not they've been spoiled for incubation and leave the nest anyhow. Killdeer are rather long-legged and have two black rings around white throats.

Lorine Niedecker

In a civilization like ours, metropolitanism intensified by machinery, human nature (which was developed under very different conditions) becomes an anachronism. We can't turn back the civilization, not at least until it collapses, and our descendants will have to develop a new sort of nature—will have to "break out of humanity"—or suffer considerably—probably both.

Robinson Jeffers

The men, though young, having tasted the first drop from the cup of thought, are already dissipated: the maples and ferns are still uncorrupt; yet no doubt, when they come to consciousness, they too will curse and swear.

Ralph Waldo Emerson

The killdeer still sitting on the eggs. The much vaunted Instinct in nature may be going astray.

Lorine Niedecker

Immortality

To have been immortal transcends to become so.

Emily Dickinson

I think we may be sure that, whatever may come after death, no one will be disappointed.

Ralph Waldo Emerson

Independence Day

England. We use her language, and receive, in torrents, the influence of her thought, yet it is, in many ways, uncongenial and injurious to our constitution. What suits Great Britain, with her insular position and consequent need to concentrate and intensify her life, her limited monarchy, and spirit of trade, does not suit a mixed race, continually enriched with new blood from other stocks the most unlike that of our first descent, with ample field and verge enough to range in and leave every impulse free, and abundant opportunity to develop a genius, wide and full as our rivers, flowery, luxuriant and impassioned as our vast prairies, rooted in strength as the rocks on which the Puritan fathers landed.

Margaret Fuller

American literature all the nineteenth century went on by itself and although it might seem to have been doing the same thing as English literature it really was not and it really was not for an excellent reason it was not leading a daily island life. Not at all nothing could be more completely not a daily island life than the life the daily life of any American. It was so completely not a daily island life that one may well say that it was not a daily life at all.

That is fundamental that is what the American writing inevitably is, it is not a daily life at all.

Gertrude Stein

Information Highway

If you chance to live and move and have your being in that thin stratum in which the events that make the news transpire,—thinner than the paper on which it is printed,—then these things will fill the world for you; but if you soar above or dive below that plane, you cannot remember nor be reminded of them. Really to see the sun rise or go down every day, so to relate ourselves to a universal fact, would preserve us sane forever. Nations! What are nations? . . . I find it so difficult to dispose of the few facts which to me are significant, that I hesitate to burden my attention with those which are insignificant, which only a divine mind could illustrate. Such is, for the most part, the news in newspapers and conversation. It is important to preserve the mind's chastity in this respect. Think of admitting the details of a single case of the criminal court into our thoughts, to stalk profanely through their very *sanctum sanctorum* for an hour, ay, for many hours! to make a very barroom of the mind's inmost apartment, as if for so long the dust of the street had occupied us,—the very street itself, with all its travel, its bustle, and filth, had passed through our thoughts' shrine! Would it not be an intellectual and moral suicide? When I have been compelled to sit spectator and auditor in a court-room for some hours, and have seen my neighbors, who were not compelled, stealing in from time to time, and tiptoeing about with washed hands and faces, it has appeared to my mind's eye, that, when they took off their hats, their ears suddenly expanded into vast hoppers for sound, between which even their narrow heads were crowded. Like the vanes of windmills, they caught the broad but shallow stream of sound, which, after a few tintillating gyrations in their coggy brains, passed out the other side. I wondered if, when they got home, they were as careful to wash their ears as before their hands and faces. It has seemed to me, at such a time, that the auditors and the witnesses, the jury and the counsel, the judge and the criminal at the bar,—if I may presume him guilty before he is convicted,—were all equally criminal, and a thunderbolt might be expected to descend and consume them all together.

By all kinds of traps and signboards, threatening the extreme penalty of the divine law, exclude such trespassers from the only ground which can be sacred to you. It is so hard to forget what it is worse than useless to remember! If I am to be a thoroughfare, I prefer that it be of mountain brooks, the Parnassian streams, and not the town sewers. There is inspiration, that gossip which comes to the ear of the attentive mind from the courts of heaven. There is the profane and stale revelation of the barroom and police court. The same ear is fitted to receive both communications. Only the character of the hearer determines to which it shall be open, and to which closed. I believe that the mind can be permanently profaned by the habit of attending to trivial things, so that all our thoughts shall be tinged with triviality. Our very intellect shall be macadamized, as it were,—its foundation broken into fragments for the wheels of travel to roll over; and if you would know what will make the most durable pavement, surpassing rolled stones, spruce blocks, and asphaltum, you have only to look into some of our minds which have been subjected to this treatment for so long.

Henry David Thoreau

Inner Resource

In a few days I go to lake Huron, and may have something to say of that region and people. From what I already see, I should say that the young native population of Canada was growing up, forming a hardy, democratic, intelligent, radically sound, and just as American, good-natured and *individualistic* race, as the average range of the best specimens among us. As among us, too, I please myself by considering that this element, though it may not be the majority, promises to be the leaven which must eventually leaven the whole lump.

Walt Whitman

If we believed in the existence of strict *individuals*, natures, that is, not radically identical but unknown, unmeasurable we should never dare to fight.

Ralph Waldo Emerson

Innocents Abroad

When much in the Woods as a little Girl, I was told that the Snake would bite me, that I might pick a poisonous flower, or Goblins kidnap me, but I went along and met no one but Angels, who were far shyer of me, than I could be of them, so I hav'nt that confidence in fraud which many exercise.

Emily Dickinson

Invisible Hand

There arose a sudden gust at N.W. so violent for half an hour, as it blew down multitudes of trees. It lifted up their meeting house at Newbury, the people being in it. It darkened the air with dust, yet through God's great mercy it did no hurt, but only killed one Indian with the fall of a tree.

John Winthrop

Isotropic Universe

All fundamental aspects of anything—moral values or an organized business activity—have their complex side; all are part of the natural laws coming up from the roots. Any man, in any valuable work—no matter how limited his capabilities and power of expression seem to him at the start—who sincerely seeks to find the truths and essentials so often confused with or covered up by the immediate and superficial, and who constantly tries, as well as he knows how, to present them in preference to the easier, the more expedient, or the less substantial, will find a way to the *kind* of success he wants. And the way will be simple enough to be understood by the many, and complex enough to be of some value to all!

Charles Ives

In town I also talked with Sampson Reed, of Swedenborg & the rest. "It is not so in your experience, but is so in the other world."—"Other world?" I reply, "there is no other world; here or nowhere is the whole fact; all the Universe over, there is but one thing—this old double, Creator-creature, mind-matter, right-wrong."

Ralph Waldo Emerson

It's a Wonderful Life

You may open a road, help start some social or business institution, contribute your mite in *any* way to the mass of the work which each generation subtracts from the task of the next; and you will come into *real* relations with your brothers—with some of them at least.

I know that in a certain point of view, and the most popular one, this seems a cold activity for our affections, a stone instead of bread. We long for sympathy, for a purely *personal* communication, first with the soul of the world, and then with the soul of our fellows. And happy are they who think, or know, that they have got them! But to those who must confess with bitter anguish that they are perfectly isolated from the soul of the world, and that the closest human love incloses a potential germ of estrangement or hatred, that all *personal* relation is finite, conditional, mixed (*vide* in Dana's "Household Book of Poetry," stanzas by C. P. Cranch, "Thought is deeper than speech," etc., etc.), it may not prove such an unfruitful substitute. At least, when you have added to the property of the race, even if no one knows your name, yet it is certain that, without what you have done, some individuals must needs be acting now in a somewhat different manner. You have modified their life; you are in *real* relation with them; you have in so far forth entered into their being. And is that such an unworthy stake to set up for our good, after all? Who are these men anyhow? Our predecessors, even apart from the physical link of generations, have made us what we are. Every thought you now have and every act and intention owes its complexion to the acts of your dead and living brothers. *Everything* we know and are is through men. We have no revelation but through man. Every sentiment that warms your gizzard, every brave act that ever made your pulse bound and your nostril open to a confident breath was a man's act. However mean a man may be, man is *the best we know*; and your loathing as you turn from what you probably call the vulgarity of human life—your homesick yearning for a *Better*, somewhere—is furnished by your manhood; your ideal is made up of traits suggested by past men's words and actions. Your manhood shuts you in forever, bounds all your thoughts like an overarching sky—and all the Good and True and High and Dear that you know by virtue of your sharing in it. They are the Natural Product of our Race. So that it seems to me that a sympathy with men as such, and a desire to contribute to the weal of a species, which, whatever may be said of it, contains All that we acknowledge as good, may very well form an external interest sufficient to keep one's moral pot boiling in a very lively manner to a good old age. The idea, in short, of becoming an accomplice in a sort of "Mankind its own God or Providence" scheme is a *practical* one.

William James

Kingdom of Heaven

Nothing is so resonant with mystery as the one that forgets us—and the boundlessness (wonder) of her—so dwarfs Heaven and Hell that we think—(recall) of them if at all, as tepid and ignoble trifles (or if we recall them it is as tepid) (or we recall) (and trifles ignoble) (It's intricacy is so boundless that it dispels Heaven and Hell)

Emily Dickinson

Land beside a House

Hope and the future for me are not in lawns and cultivated fields, not in towns and cities, but in the impervious and quaking swamps. When, formerly, I have analyzed my partiality for some farm which I had contemplated purchasing, I have frequently found that I was attracted solely by a few square rods of impermeable and unfathomable bog,—a natural sink in one corner of it. That was the jewel which dazzled me. I derive more of my subsistence from the swamps which surround my native town than from the cultivated gardens in the village. There are no richer parterres to my eyes than the dense beds of dwarf andromeda (*Cassandra calyculata*) which cover these tender places on the earth's surface. Botany cannot go farther than tell me the names of the shrubs which grow there,—the high blueberry, panicled andromeda, lamb-kill, azalea, and rhodora,—all standing in the quaking sphagnum. I often think that I should like to have my house front on this mass of dull red bushes, omitting other flower plots and borders, transplanted spruce and trim box, even graveled walks,—to have this fertile spot under my windows, not a few imported barrowfuls of soil only to cover the sand which was thrown out in digging the cellar. Why not put my house, my parlor, behind this plot, instead of behind that meager assemblage of curiosities, that poor apology for a Nature and Art, which I call my front yard? It is an effort to clear up and make a decent appearance when the carpenter and the mason have departed, though done as much for the passer-by as for the dweller within. The most tasteful front-yard fence was never

an agreeable object of study to me; the most elaborate orna-
ments, acorn tops, or what not, soon wearied and disgusted
me. Bring your sills up to the very edge of the swamp, then
(though it may not be the best place for a dry cellar), so that
there be no access on that side to citizens. Front yards are not
made to walk in, but, at most, through, and you could go in
the back way.

Henry David Thoreau

Land Ethic

You say you "feel strongly that this country has not been loved
enough inch by inch." I agree, but I would put it differ-
ently. . . . I think that this country has been taken too much
for granted, the country geologically, botanically, as well as its
creatures, all of them. From this it follows that no one pays
attention to it. My best painting comes as a surprise to me
because I literally do not know whether something is "beauti-
ful" or whether I "love" it. . . . You can only buck generalities
by attention to facts. So aesthetics is what connects one to
matters of fact. It is anti–ideal, it is materialistic. It implies no
approval, but *respect* for things as they are. America inch by
inch. This has nothing to do with evaluation or usefulness.
Technology, on the other hand, has only to do with evaluation
and usefulness. Technology is what threatens life on this
planet. It is idealism put into practice.

Fairfield Porter

Chief Sleepy Eyes rose when the meeting began, "Father, your
coming and asking me for my country makes me sad; and
your saying that I am not able to do anything with my country
makes me still more sad."

Lorine Niedecker

I saw the Sacs & Foxes at the Statehouse on Monday—about
30 in number. Edward Everett addressed them & they re-
plied. One chief said "They had no land to put their words
upon, but they were nevertheless true."

Ralph Waldo Emerson

Library of America

When Flowers annually died and I was a child, I used to read Dr Hitckcock's Book on the Flowers of North America. This comforted their Absence—assuring me they lived.

Emily Dickinson

Life Studies

My own autobiography has never interested me very much. Whenever I try to think about it, I seem to draw a complete blank.

John Ashbery

Literary Theory

You cannot imagine the size of a place like Arizona and its neighbor, New Mexico nor the effect of that size on the validity of French poets in general.

Wallace Stevens

I cannot divest my appetite of literature, yet I find myself eventually trying it all by Nature—*first premises* many call it, but really the crowning results of all, laws, tallies and proofs. (Has it never occurr'd to any one how the last deciding tests applicable to a book are entirely outside of technical and grammatical ones, and that any truly first-class production has little or nothing to do with the rules and calibres of ordinary critics? or the bloodless chalk of Allibone's Dictionary? I have fancied the ocean and the daylight, the mountain and the forest, putting their spirit in a judgment on our books. I have fancied some disembodied human soul giving its verdict.)

Walt Whitman

Taurus: Lorine Niedecker. *Gemini*: Ralph Waldo Emerson, Margaret Fuller, Walt Whitman, Rachel Carson, Fairfield Porter.

Cancer: Henry David Thoreau. *Leo*: John Wise, John Ashbery. *Virgo*: William Carlos Williams. *Libra*: Jonathan Edwards, Charles Ives, Wallace Stevens. *Scorpio*: Marianne Moore, James Schuyler. *Sagittarius*: Emily Dickinson. *Capricorn*: William James, Aldo Leopold, Robinson Jeffers. *Aquarius*: Gertrude Stein, Langston Hughes. *Pisces*: Liberty Hyde Bailey, W. E. B. Du Bois.

We have much that we call nature poetry, but most of it will not be nature poetry in the time to come.

Liberty Hyde Bailey

Love

If you saw a bullet hit a Bird—and he told you he was'nt shot—you might weep at his courtesy, but you would certainly doubt his word.

Emily Dickinson

And now another friendship has ended. I do not know what has made my friend doubt me, but I know that in love there is no mistake, and that every estrangement is well founded. But my destiny is not narrowed, but if possible the broader for it. The heavens withdraw and arch themselves higher. I am sensible not only of a moral, but even a grand physical pain, such as gods may feel, about my head and breast, a certain ache and fullness. This rending of a tie, it is not my work nor thine. It is no accident that we mind; it is only the awards of fate that are affecting. I know of no eons, or periods, no life and death, but these meetings and separations. My life is like a stream that is suddenly dammed and has no outlet; but it rises the higher up the hills that shut it in, and will become a deep and silent lake. Certainly there is no event comparable for grandeur with the eternal separation—if we may conceive it so—from a being that we have known. I become in a degree sensible of the meaning of finite and infinite. What a grand significance the word "never" acquires!

Henry David Thoreau

57

I could better have the earth taken away from under my feet, than the thought of you from my mind.

Henry David Thoreau

Yet Tenderness has not a Date—it comes—and overwhelms.

Emily Dickinson

Love It or Leave It

I am sitting in a 60-mile-an-hour bus sailing over a highway originally laid out for horse and buggy. The ribbon of concrete has been widened and widened until the field fences threaten to topple into the road cuts. In the narrow thread of sod between the shaved banks and the toppling fences grow the relics of what once was Illinois: the prairie.

No one in the bus sees these relics. A worried farmer, his fertilizer bill projecting from his pocket, looks blankly at the lupines, lespedezas, or Baptisias that originally pumped nitrogen out of the prairie air and into his black loamy acres. He does not distinguish them from the parvenu quack-grass in which they grow. Were I to ask him why his corn makes a hundred bushels, while that of non-prairie states does well to make thirty, he would probably answer that Illinois soil is better. Were I to ask him the name of that white spike of pea-like flowers hugging the fence, he would shake his head. A weed, likely. . . .

The highway stretches like a taut tape across the corn, oats, and clover fields; the bus ticks off the opulent miles; the passengers talk and talk and talk. About what? About baseball, taxes, sons-in-law, movies, motors, and funerals, but never about the groundswell of Illinois that washes the windows of the speeding bus. Illinois has no genesis, no history, no shoals or deeps, no tides of life and death. To them Illinois is only the sea on which they sail to ports unknown.

Aldo Leopold

Majority Rule

Dear friends—we cannot believe for each other.

Emily Dickinson

The Making of Americans

The whole object of the universe to us is the formation of character. If you think you came into being for the purpose of taking an important part in the administration of events, to guard a province of the moral creation from ruin, and that its salvation hangs on the success of your single arm, you have wholly mistaken your business.

Ralph Waldo Emerson

It [culture] must have for its spinal meaning the formation of a typical personality of character, eligible to the uses of the high average of men—and not restricted by conditions ineligible to the masses.

Walt Whitman

In a great many educations in a great many countries they want one lot of them to be a very different lot from the other lot. Do we. I wonder. Do we.

Gertrude Stein

Manifest Destiny

The evolution-conception of the universe bids us come and stand on a high place. It magnifies individual effort, kindles the inner light of conscience in distinction from authority, lessens belief in mere wonders, stimulates the reason, and emancipates the man. It asks us to lay aside prejudice and small dogmatisms. It impels us to a new and great reverence for the Power which has set in motion that stupendous enterprise which unfolds itself without a break or change of purpose, setting the stars in their courses and molding the strawberry into its new environments, losing no detail in its mighty swing and running on to destiny in ages hence of which we cannot yet perceive the meaning. It bids us put ourselves in line with the movements of the ages, to throw aside all mental reservation and oppositions to truth, and to do our little, with sympathy and inspiration, to forward the creation. All beliefs, all doctrines, all creeds are mine. I want only the truth and the privilege to live in the great good world. Truth, and the quest for truth, are always safe. It is not my part to be anxious about destiny or about the universe. If my tiny opinions are out-grown, I shall wait, in patience and hope. There is grateful release in letting the universe take care of itself.

Liberty Hyde Bailey

As for compliments, even the stars praise me, and I praise them. . . . When I hear praise coming, do I not elevate and arch myself to hear it like the sky, and as impersonally? Think I appropriate any of it to my weak legs? No. Praise away *till all is blue*.

Henry David Thoreau

"I have fallen in love outward" [means] the feeling—I will say the certitude—that the world, the universe, is one being, a single organism, one great life that includes all life and all things, and is so beautiful it must be loved and reverenced, and in moments of mystical vision we identify ourselves with it.

Robinson Jeffers

There is nothing between us & the infinite Universe.
Ralph Waldo Emerson

Materials and Methods

Odd as it may seem that a few words of overwhelming ur-gency should be a mosaic of quotations, why paraphrase what for maximum impact should be quoted verbatim?

Marianne Moore

The Media

Remember Sojourner Truth, the large negro slave woman who was illiterate but went about speech making?—her only income was from pictures of herself which she sold. She said, "I sells the shadow to support the substance."

Lorine Niedecker

It is difficult to believe but it is true, I had never heard a broadcasting; that is I had never listened to one before and I had certainly never thought of doing one, and this is the way the thing that I like best of all the things I have never done before, was done. They said would I and I of course said I would. I never say no, not in America.

The first thing they did was to photograph me doing it, not doing it but making believe doing it, this was easily done. There was nothing natural or unnatural about that.

And then we went into training. I liked that; I wrote out answers to questions and questions to answers and I liked that, and then one day the day had come, and it was to be done.

We went there, there were so many rooms and all the rooms were empty rooms, that was all right; then all of a sudden we were in a little room, and they were going to time us and they did. That seemed to me very well done, they knew so well how to do this thing and no fuss was made about anything, and then I was taken into another room and there there were more people but by that time I was not noticing much of anything.

Then we sat down one on either side of the little thing that was between us and I said something and they said that is all, and then suddenly it was all going on. It was it was really all going on, and it was, it really was, as if you were saying what you were saying and you knew, you really knew, not by what you knew but by what you felt, that everybody was listening. It is a very wonderful thing to do, I almost stopped and said it, I was so filled with it. And then it was over and I never had liked anything as I had liked it.

This then was the last completion, of what is, that is that the unreal is natural, so natural that it makes of unreality the most natural of anything natural. That is what America does, and that is what America is. Long ago, oh way long ago, long before I had ever dreamed these things that prove it, I said, that what made America and American literature was a quality of being disembodied, and I said there was Emerson, and there was Hawthorne and there was Edgar Poe and there was Walt Whitman and there was, well, in a funny way there was Mark Twain and then there was Henry James and then there was—well, there is—well, I am. So you see one follows the other and they are all, well, they are all abstract if you know what I mean, and the color is, and the land is, and the buildings are, and everything is, and so and so the red Indian was, and is.

Gertrude Stein

A camera! a camera! cries the century, that is the only toy.

Ralph Waldo Emerson

Modern Times

Passionless and fixed, at the six-stroke the boats come in; and at the three-stroke, succeeded by a single tap, they depart again, with the steadiness of nature herself. Perhaps a man, prompted by the hell-like delirium tremens, has jumped overboard and been drowned: still the trips go on as before. Perhaps someone has been crushed between the landing and the prow—(ah! that most horrible thing of all!) still, no matter, for the great business of the mass must be helped forward as before. A moment's pause—the quick gathering of a curious crowd, (how strange that they can look so unshudderingly on the scene!)—the paleness of the more chicken-hearted— and all subsides, and the current sweeps as it did the moment previously. How it deadens one's sympathies, this living in a city!

Walt Whitman

The Mother of Us All

Nature is lush here, I feel as tho I spent my childhood outdoors—redwinged blackbirds, willows, maples, boats, fishing (the smell of tarred nets), tittering and squawking noises from the marsh.

Lorine Niedecker

We were walking along the beach at sunset, heading for a cocktail party. The sun was casting those extraordinary Technicolor effects on the sea and sky. John turned to me and said, "I always feel so embarrassed by these gaudy displays of nature." I didn't feel embarrassed at all.

James Schuyler

Is it not a bit beside the point for us to be so solicitous about preserving institutions without giving so much as a thought to preserving the environment which produced them and which may now be one of our effective means of keeping them alive?

Aldo Leopold

National Endowment

An American Protestant, who has no experience of art, and consequently no artistic standards, finds his artistic standards in what to him is closest to art, and a little less strange, namely religion. (Perhaps this is also the reason why esthetics is often confused with ethics in America.) He fills the esthetic gap with a humorless attention to boring detail. He paints as if he were Abraham Lincoln walking miles to return three cents change.

Fairfield Porter

National Guard

Fellow Citizens, in these times full of the fate of the Republic, I think the towns should hold town meetings, and resolve themselves into Committees of Safety, go into permanent sessions, adjourning from week to week, month to month. I wish we could send the Sergeant-at-arms to stop every American who is about to leave the country. Send home every one who is abroad, lest they should find no country to return to. Come home and stay at home, while there is a country to save. When it is lost it will be time enough then for any who are luckless enough to remain alive to gather up their clothes and depart to some land where freedom exists.

Ralph Waldo Emerson

As a group of citizens calling to our country to return to the principles which it was suckled in, I believe that we Anti-Imperialists are already a back number. We had better not print that name upon our publications any longer. The country has once for all regurgitated the Declaration of Independence and the Farewell Address, and it won't swallow again immediately what it is so happy to have vomited up. It has come to a hiatus. It has deliberately pushed itself into the circle of international hatreds, and joined the common pack of wolves. It relishes the attitude. We have thrown off our swaddling clothes, it thinks, and attained our majority. We are objects of fear to other lands. This makes of the old liberalism and the new liberalism of our country two discontinuous things. The older liberalism was in office, the new is in the opposition. Inwardly it is the same spirit, but outwardly the tactics, the questions, the reasons, and the phrases have to change. American memories no longer serve as catchwords. The great international and cosmopolitan liberal party, the party of conscience and intelligence the world over, has, in short, absorbed us; and we are only its American section, carrying on the war against the powers of darkness here, playing our part in the long, long campaign for truth and fair dealing which must go on in all the countries of the world until the end of time. Let us cheerfully settle into our interminable task. Everywhere it is the same struggle under various names,—light against darkness, right against might, love against hate. The Lord of life is with us, and we cannot permanently fail.

William James

Native Tongue

Prospecting thus the coming unsped days, and that new or-
der in them—marking the endless train of exercise, develop-
ment, unwind, in nation as well as in man, which life is for—
we see, fore-indicated, amid these prospects and hopes, new
law-forces of spoken and written language—not merely the
pedagogue-forms, correct, regular, familiar with precedents,
made for matters of outside propriety, fine words, thoughts
definitely told out—but a language fann'd by the breath of
Nature, which leaps overhead, cares mostly for impetus and
effects, and for what it plants and invigorates to grow—
tallies life and character, and seldomer tells a thing than
suggests or indicates it.

Walt Whitman

Clarity is of no importance because nobody listens and no-
body knows what you mean no matter what you mean, nor
how clearly you mean what you mean. But if you have vitality
enough of knowing enough of what you mean, somebody and
sometime and sometimes a great many will have to realize that
you know what you mean and so they will agree that you
mean what you know, what you know you mean, which is as
near as anybody can come to understanding anyone.

Gertrude Stein

Sometimes, when I am writing a thing, it is complete in my
own mind; I write it in my own way and don't care what
happens. I don't mean to say that I am deliberately obscure,
but I do mean to say that, when the thing has been put down
and is complete to my own way of thinking, I let it go. After
all, if the thing is really there, the reader gets it. He may not
get it at once, but, if he is sufficiently interested, he invariably
gets it. A man who wrote with the idea of being deliberately
obscure would be an imposter. But that is not the same thing
as a man who allows a difficult thing to remain difficult be-
cause, if he explained it, it would, to his way of thinking,
destroy it.

Wallace Stevens

The notes hold into the next general thought, as thoughts do—every thought hasn't a clothes-pin between it—they go on and up. Emerson's thought was usually a part of the before and afterward—not little miniature ideas in frames, to be read easily and put down, etc. It was bigger and greater and higher than a one-line picture on paper. These longer notes on the lesser beats, of course, are helped by the pedal, but ped . . . * underneath is a poor substitute for what I had in mind—(that is, what Emerson, Thoreau, etc. had in mind, and what I tried to get out of my system in "tones" or in "sounds" if you like—call it music or not, it makes no difference)—and then the pedal, unless used in long or whole-phrase passages, when lifted, stops the thought-sounds, which ought to be thought of continuing to their natural ends. So to write them, usually the more fundamental themes, somewhat in this way is nearer to what the music (?) should be to the ear and the in-mind than the limited but more conventional (more proper) way. In fact, as soon as music goes down on paper, it loses something of its birthright!

Charles Ives

Things are in a continual state of motion and evolution, and if we come to a point where we say, with certitude, right here, this is the end of the universe, then of course we must deal with everything that goes on after that, whereas ambiguity seems to take further developments into account.

John Ashbery

The following principles . . . are aids to composition by which I try, myself, to be guided: if a long sentence with dependent clauses seems obscure, one can break it into shorter units by imagining into what phrases it would fall as conversation; in the second place, expanded explanation tends to spoil the lion's leap—an awkwardness which is surely brought home to one in conversation; and in the third place, we must be as clear as our natural reticence allows us to be.

Marianne Moore

Tongue II

America is funny that way everything is quick but really everybody does move slowly, and the movement of the oil well that slow movement very well that slow movement is the country and it makes it prehistoric and large shapes and moving slowly very very slowly so slowly that they do almost stand still. I do think Americans are slow minded, it seems quick but they are slow minded yes they are.

Gertrude Stein

Natural Law

The idea of right exists in the human mind, and lays itself out in the equilibrium of Nature, in the equalities and periods of our system, in the level of seas, in the action and reaction of forces. Nothing is allowed to exceed or absorb the rest; if it do, it is disease, and quickly destroyed. It was an early discovery of the mind,—this beneficent rule.

Ralph Waldo Emerson

A thing is right when it tends to preserve the integrity, stability, and beauty of the biotic community. It is wrong when it tends otherwise.

Aldo Leopold

Nature

How many animals birds wild flowers are there in the United States and is it splendid of it to have any.

Gertrude Stein

New York

I very frequently used to retire into a solitary place, on the banks of Hudson's river, at some distance from the city, for contemplation on divine things and secret converse with God, and had many sweet hours there. . . . I went from New York to Weathersfield by water. As I sailed away, I kept sight of the city as long as I could, and when I was out of sight of it, it would affect me much to look that way, with a kind of melancholy mixed with sweetness.

Jonathan Edwards

There is no thrill in all the world like entering, for the first time, New York harbor,—coming in from the flat monotony of the sea to this rise of dreams and beauty.

Langston Hughes

New York is the focus, the point where American and European interests converge. . . . Twenty months have presented me with a richer and more varied exercise for thought and life, than twenty years could in any other part of these United States.

Margaret Fuller

I wanted to be in New York, I had to be in Washington: I was never in the one place but I was restless for the other: my heart was distracted.

Walt Whitman

No: New York is not the world. Yet one says it of New York with less assurance than one says it of Hartford.

Wallace Stevens

Nothing happens in the city. Everything happens in the country. The city just tells what has happened in the country, it has already happened in the country.
    Lizzie do you understand.

Gertrude Stein

No Ideas but in Things

The child should be taught to understand *things*, as well as *words*.

Jonathan Edwards

Knowledge is the thing you know and how can you know more than you do know.

Gertrude Stein

From every point of view, the overwhelming and portentous character ascribed to universal conceptions is surprising. Why, from Plato and Aristotle downwards, philosophers should have vied with each other in scorn of the knowledge of the particular and in adoration of that of the general, is hard to understand, seeing that the more adorable knowledge ought to be that of the more adorable things and that the things of worth are all concretes and singulars. The only value of universal characters is that they help us, by reasoning, to know new truths about individual things. The restriction of one's meaning, moreover, to an individual thing probably requires even more complicated brain-processes than its extension to all the instances of a kind; and the mere mystery, as such, of the knowledge is equally great, whether generals or singulars be the thing known. In sum, the traditional universal-worship can only be called a bit of perverse sentimentalism.

William James

At the very moment when abstract thinking seems about to produce a result, something concrete steps in and takes its place.

John Ashbery

As the attributes of the poets of the kosmos concentre in the real body and soul and in the pleasure of things they possess the superiority of genuineness over all fiction and romance. As they emit themselves facts are showered over with light. . . .

Walt Whitman

And I realized after such a long acquaintanceship that his [Porter's] paintings, which most people like but have difficulty talking about (are they modern enough? too French? too pleasant? hasn't this been done before?), are part of the intellectual fabric that underlay his opinions, his conversation, his poetry, his way of being. They are intellectual in the classic American tradition . . . because they have no ideas in them, that is, no ideas that can be separated from the rest.

John Ashbery

A deep insight will always, like Nature, ultimate its thought in a thing.*

Ralph Waldo Emerson

The One Thing that Can Save America

The true gravitation-hold of liberalism in the United States will be a more universal ownership of property, general homesteads, general comfort—a vast, intertwining reticulation of wealth. . . . So that, from another point of view, ungracious as it may sound, and a paradox after what we have been saying, democracy looks with suspicious, ill-satisfied eye upon the very poor, the ignorant, and on those out of business. She asks for men and women with occupations, well-off, owners of houses and acres, and with cash in the bank—and with some cravings for literature, too; and must have them, and hastens to make them.

Walt Whitman

G.I.s and G.I.s and G.I.s and they have made me come all over patriotic. I was always patriotic, I was always in my way a Civil War veteran, but in between, there were other things, but now there are no other things. And I am sure that this particular moment in our history is more important than anything since the Civil War. We are there where we have to have to fight a spiritual pioneer fight or we will go poor as England

---

*Lost in Translation

It hardly required much power of mind to see . . . that "No ideas but in things," the slogan Williams was so proud of, represents a consummation devoutly not to be wished, supposing it to be possible (as fortunately it isn't).
—Donald Davie, April 20, 1987 [The late Professor Davie was English.]

and other industrial countries have gone poor, and dont think that communism or socialism will save you, you just have to find a new way, you have to find out how you can go ahead without running away with yourselves, you have to learn to produce without exhausting your country's wealth, you have to learn to be individual and not just mass job workers, you have to get courage enough to know what you feel and not just all be yes or no men, but you have to really learn to express complication, go easy and if you cant go easy go as easy as you can. Remember the depression, dont be afraid to look it in the face and find out the reason why, dont be afraid of the reason why, if you dont find out the reason why you'll go poor and my God how I would hate to have my native land go poor. Find out the reason why, look facts in the face, not just what they all say, the leaders, but every darn one of you so that a government by the people for the people shall not perish from the face of the earth, it wont, somebody else will do it if we lie down on the job, but of all things dont stop, find out the reason why of the depression, find it out each and every one of you and then look the facts in the face. We are Americans.

Gertrude Stein

Early maps with emphasized shore-lines and rivers have much in common with the modern air-view. Though the photograph may seem as art somewhat "easier," both styles of likeness confer unrealistic distinction, so that New York as foreshortened in a view taken recently by The Airmap Corporation of America, wears the delicately engraved aspect of a sand-dollar or cluster of barnacles. Our master-production, The Clifford Milburn Holland Vehicular Tunnel, is not visible. In close approach to entrance or exit it is scarcely more perceptible than a wormhole, but pourings of traffic toward Broome Street or from Canal Street indicate sand-dollar selfhelpfulness within and encourage one to feel that occupancy will presently have become indigenous i.e. that the tunnel will presently have paid for itself and be free to the public. We are glad to have civic prowess subjacent. Expenditure does not seem expenditure when the result is a benefit.

Marianne Moore

Original Intent

If the Bill of Rights contains no guarantee that a citizen shall be secure against lethal poisons distributed either by private individuals or by public officials, it is surely only because our forefathers, despite their considerable wisdom and foresight, could conceive of no such problem.

Rachel Carson

Do you suppose the world is finished, at any certain time— like a contract for paving a street?—Do you suppose because the American government has been formed, and public schools established, we have nothing more to do but take our ease, and make money, and sleep out the rest of the time?

Walt Whitman

Original Position

Till it has loved—no man or woman can become itself—Of our first Creation we are unconscious—

Emily Dickinson

Over There

After all, would one really go to Europe to enjoy life if one had the choice nowadays? I don't mean pictures or books or Paris. Wouldn't one just as lief go to some of the blesseder spots over here where there would be no risk of being suddenly ossified by the stare of an Englishman?

Wallace Stevens

Our people creep abroad that they may ruffle it at home.

Ralph Waldo Emerson

Pair Bond

I have discovered that the thrill of first love passes! It even becomes the backbone of a sordid sort of religion if not assisted in passing. I knew a man who kept a candle burning before a girl's portrait day and night for a year—then jilted her, pawned her off on a friend. I have been reasonably frank about my erotics with my wife. I have never or seldom said, my dear I love you, when I would rather say: My dear, I wish you were in Tierra del Fuego. I have discovered by scrupulous attention to this detail and by certain allied experiments that we can continue from time to time to elaborate relationships quite equal in quality, if not greatly superior, to that surrounding our wedding. In fact, the best we have enjoyed of love together has come after the most thorough destruction or harvesting of that which has gone before. Periods of barrenness have intervened, periods comparable to the prison music in *Fidelio* or to any of Beethoven's pianissimo transition passages. It is at these times our formal relations have teetered on the edge of a debacle to be followed, as our imaginations have permitted, by a new growth of passionate attachment dissimilar in every member to that which has gone before.

William Carlos Williams

Mrs. Stevens and I went out for a walk yesterday afternoon. We walked to the end of Westerly Terrace, and she turned left and I turned right.

Wallace Stevens

Patriotic Songs

We have had two peerless summer days after all our cold winds & rains. I have weeded corn & strawberries, intent on being fat & have forborne study. The Maryland yellow-throat pipes to me all day long, seeming to say extacy! Extacy! . . .

Ralph Waldo Emerson

And when all is still at night, the owls take up their strain, like mourning women their ancient ululu. . . . They give me a new sense of the vastness and mystery of nature which is the common dwelling of us both. "Oh-o-o-o-o that I had never been bor-or-or-or-orn!" sighs one on this side of the pond, and circles in the restlessness of despair to some new perch in the gray oaks. Then "That I had never been bor-or-or-or-orn!" echoes one on the further side, with a tremendous sincerity, and "Bor-or-or-or-orn" comes faintly from far in the Lincoln woods.

Henry David Thoreau

Pledge of Allegiance

This is what you shall do: Love the earth and sun and the animals, despise riches, give alms to every one that asks, stand up for the stupid and crazy, devote your income and labor to others, hate tyrants, argue not concerning God, have patience and indulgence toward the people, take off your hat to nothing known or unknown or to any man or number of men, go freely with powerful uneducated persons and with the young and with the mothers of families, read these leaves in the open air every season of every year of your life, re-examine all you have been told at school or church or in any book, dismiss whatever insults your own soul, and your flesh shall be a great poem and have the richest fluency not only in its words but in the silent lines of its lips and face and between the lashes of your eyes and in every motion and joint of your body.

Walt Whitman

Poetry

This is a time for the highest poetry. We never understood the world less than we do now nor, as we understand it, liked it less. We never wanted to understand it more or needed to like it more. These are the intense compulsions that challenge the poet as the appreciatory creator of values and beliefs. That, finally, states the problem.

Wallace Stevens

Poetry II

Will it help breed one goodshaped and wellhung man, and a woman to be his perfect and independent mate?

Walt Whitman

Poetry and Prose

If I read a book it makes my whole body so cold no fire ever can warm me I know *that* is poetry. If I feel physically as if the top of my head were taken off, I know *that* is poetry. These are the only way I know it. Is there any other way.

Emily Dickinson

Is not poetry the little chamber in the brain where is generated the explosive force which, by gentle shocks, sets in action the intellectual world?

Ralph Waldo Emerson

What is poetry and if you know what poetry is what is prose.

Gertrude Stein

Poetry is a magic of pauses, as a dog-valentine contrasting *pawses* and *pauses*—sent to me from Harvard where I had been discussing pauses—reminded me. I do not know what syllabic verse is. I find no appropriate application for it.

Marianne Moore

It is conceivable that what is unified form to the author or composer may of necessity be formless to his audience. A home run will cause more unity in the grandstand than in the season's batting average. If a composer once starts to compromise, his work will begin to drag on *him*.

Charles Ives

A friend of mine, Arthur Gold, a man I once lived with, encouraged me to try writing in the formal styles, so I did for

75

a little while—this irritated John Ashbery very much, who once said, "Have you written anything lately that would interest me?"

James Schuyler

I find one can say very much more by advancing immediately to the poetry in the poem.

John Ashbery

All the interest that you feel in occasional frivolities I seem to experience in sounds, and many lines exist because I enjoy their clickety-clack in contrast with the more decorous pom-pom-pom that people expect.

Wallace Stevens

Poetry Reading

It is not easy to appear spiritual and poetic before a thousand children at the crack of dawn.

Langston Hughes

Profiles in Courage

There are communities—now partly vanished, but cherished and sacred—scattered throughout this world of ours, in which freedom of thought and soul, and even of body, have been fought for. And we believe that there lives in that part of the over-soul native to them the thoughts which these freedom-struggles have inspired. America is not too young to have its divinities, and its place-legends.

Charles Ives

Sam Patch

In his late teens, Patch gained local fame as a daredevil in Pawtucket, Rhode Island, where he was employed in a cotton mill, by dropping feet first into the Blackstone River from the top of a high building. He first appeared as a professional leaper in Paterson, New Jersey, and moved from there to Niagara Falls, where twice he jumped into the white and agitated waters below the cataract. . . . When he arrived in Rochester with his bear and his pet fox, he lost no time in getting out handbills and posters. . . . ANOTHER LEAP! SAM PATCH AGAINST THE WORLD, the *Rochester Daily Advertiser* announced in its October 29 [1829] issue.

Then followed one of Sam's maxims which soon got into the idiom: "Some things can be done as well as others."

The Genesee

In defiance of fate he chose Friday the 13th as the day for his second leap. To make the stunt more spectacular, he was to leap from a wooden scaffold 25 feet above the 100-foot height of the verge of the Falls. The newspapers gave wide publicity to the event. Special schooners ran excursions from Oswego and from Canadian towns. Hundreds of farmers traveled the muddy roads leading to the Falls. More than 8,000 people, shivering in the cold of that bleak November day, crowded along the river to see Sam Patch leap.

WPA Guide to Rochester and Monroe County

"And who was Sam Patch?"

"Isabel, your ignorance of all that an American woman should be proud of distresses me. Have you really, then, never heard of the man who invented the saying, 'Some things can be done as well as others,' and proved it by jumping over Niagara Falls twice? Spurred on by this belief, he attempted the leap of the Genesee Falls. The leap was easy enough, but the coming up again was another matter. He failed in that. It was the one thing that could not be done as well as others."

Their Wedding Journey

Sojourner Truth

Born sometime shortly after 1790, this woman, who was six feet tall, gained her freedom from bondage in New York State in the early 1820's, dropped her given name and started westward on a "sojourn to preach truth." Her crusade against slavery took her into tiny halls and spacious legislative chambers, into humble shacks and the office of President Lincoln. She came to Battle Creek, an abolitionist stronghold, in 1858.

WPA Guide to Michigan

"I will speak upon the ashes," she said when Indiana opponents planned to burn one meetinghouse. In a more famous instance, she spoke so powerfully in 1858 that a doctor in the audience challenged her to prove she was not a man in woman's clothing. Speaking of the white children she had nursed in slavery, she unbuttoned her dress, telling the crowd it was to their shame, not hers.

Battle Creek: The Place Behind the Products

A series of women's conventions in various parts of the country followed the one at Seneca Falls. At one of these ... was Sojourner Truth. "That man over there says that woman needs to be helped into carriages and lifted over ditches. Nobody ever helps me into carriages, or over mud-puddles or gives me any best place. And a'nt I a woman? Look at my arm! I have ploughed, and planted and gathered into barns, and no man could head me! And a'nt I a woman? I have borne thirteen children and seen em most all sold off to slavery, and when I cried out with my mother's grief, none but Jesus heard me! And a'nt I a woman?"

A People's History of the United States

John Wise

A boat's crew from his parish were captured by pirates on our coast. When beseeching the Lord on a Sabbath morning, to give them speedy deliverance, he said, "Great God! if there is no other way, may they rise, and butcher their enemies." The next day, the men arrived and related, that, the very morning before, they had attacked the pirates and killed them.—In person, Mr. Wise was of a majestic form, and of great muscular strength and activity. When young and before his ordination, he was accounted a superior wrestler. Such repute was much more respectable in his day than in ours.

History of Ipswich, Essex, and Hamilton, Mass.

Perhaps the reason for his uniqueness lies in the fact that he was the son of an indentured servant: at least, it is tempting to think so. Somehow he managed to go to Harvard, graduating in 1673. He was ordained in 1682 at the Chebacco parish, a corner of Ipswich township. He led the town in fiery protest against taxes levied in 1687 by Governor Andros without the consent of any legislature. In 1690 he was the chaplain of the disastrous expedition against Quebec; he helped check the witchcraft panic, supported inoculation in 1721, and in his last years, in sharp contrast to others of the ministerial caste, he advocated paper money.

The American Puritans

1770—Boston Massacre. *1772*—Rev. John Wise's famous "Vindication of the Government of New England Churches," first published in 1717, is republished to become the "bible" of the patriots and a reaffirmation of a man's "rights to life, liberty, estate and honor"—ideas which soon became part of the Declaration of Independence.

Three Hundred & Fifty Years of Ipswich History

Why does one not hear Americans speak more often of these important things?

Because the fools do not believe they have sprung from anything: bone, thought and action. They will not see that what they are is growing on these roots. They will not look. They float without question. Their history is to them an enigma.

What superb beauty! As with all histories, it begins with giants—cruel, but enormous, who ate flesh. They were giants.

William Carlos Williams

The Public and Its Problems

It is the fashion of a certain set to despise "politics" and the "corruption of parties" and the unmanageableness of the masses: they look at the fierce struggle, and at the battle of principles and candidates, and their weak nerves retreat dismayed from the neighborhood of such scenes of convulsion. But to our view, the spectacle is always a grand one. . . . Is it too much to feel this joy that among *us* the *whole surface* of the body politic is expanded to the sun and air, and each man feels his rights and *acts* them? . . . We know well enough that the workings of Democracy are not always justifiable, in every trivial point. But the great winds that purify the air, and with-

out which nature would flag into ruin—are they to be con-
demned because a tree is prostrated here and there, in their
course?

Walt Whitman

We were proud of the people and believed they would not go
down from this height. But peace came, and every one ran
back into his shop again, and can hardly be won to patriotism
more, even to the point of chasing away the thieves that are
stealing not only the public gold, but the newly won rights of
the slave, and the new muzzles we had contrived to keep the
planter from sucking his blood.

Ralph Waldo Emerson

Those of us engaged in this racial struggle in America are like
knights on horseback—the Negroes on a white horse and the
white folks on a black. Sometimes the race is terrific. But the
feel of the wind in your hair as you ride toward democracy is
really something! And the air smells so good!

Langston Hughes

Publish or Perish

To those to whom we owe affection, let us be dumb until we
are strong, though we should never be strong. I hate mumped
and measled lovers.

Ralph Waldo Emerson

Had we less to say to those we love, perhaps we should say it
oftener, but the attempt comes, then the inundation, then it is
all over, as is said of the dead.

Emily Dickinson

Pursuit of Happiness

Life consists in what a man is thinking of all day.

Ralph Waldo Emerson

Naturally if you want to sell things your mind must be empty of everything except the thing to be sold if you want to buy and make things your mind must necessarily be full of a great many things in other words a mind that is full of many things chooses but a mind that is full of only one thing has to go on selling that thing and not choosing anything.

All this has a great deal to do with why American men feel as they do they do not feel anything is anything if they are not actively engaged in selling something and it is easy to begin selling something young and so generally speaking those colleges where the young men and young women are determined to be ones going to be going to be selling something than making or buying or giving something naturally give this impression of being young, both men and women. If you think about it you will see what I mean. I do not wish to mention anything but I do wish to say everything.

Undoubtedly then American men feel that they must be destined to sell anything and if they are to sell anything must they not be young and if they must be young must they not have the education that being young is inculcating and must they then not naturally very naturally not wish to be feeling or thinking about anything in general.

Gertrude Stein

To live in Cuba, to think a little in the morning and afterward to work in the garden for an hour or two, then to have lunch and to read all afternoon and then, with your wife or someone else's wife, fill the house with fresh roses, to play a little Berlioz (this is the current combination at home: Berlioz and roses) might very well create all manner of doubts after a week or two. But when you are a little older, and have your business or your job to look after, and when there is quite enough to worry about all the time, and when you don't have time to think and the weeds grow in the garden a good deal more savagely than you could ever have supposed, and you no longer read because it doesn't seem worth while, but you do at the end of the day play a record or two, that is something quite different. Reality is the great *fond*, and it is because it is that the purely literary amounts to so little. Moreover, in the world of actuality, in spite of all I have just said, one is always living a little out of it. There is a precious sentence in Henry James, for whom everyday life was not much more than the mere business of living, but, all the same, he separated himself from it. The sentence is . . .

> "To live *in* the world of creation—to get into it and stay in it—to frequent it and haunt it—to think intensely and fruitfully—to woo combinations and inspirations into being by a depth and continuity of attention and meditation—this is the only thing."

Wallace Stevens

Ambiguity seems to be the same thing as happiness or pleasant surprise. I am assuming that from the moment life cannot be one continual orgasm, real happiness is impossible, and pleasant surprise is promoted to the front rank of the emotions.

John Ashbery

Quiet Desperation

Of course I know, as well as anybody that he who verbally celebrates and glorifies a function writes himself down for the time as one who doesn't exercise it, but aspires toward it rather, and seeks to animate himself and keep his courage up. . . . Heroism is always on a precipitous edge, and only keeps alive by running. Every moment is an *escape*. And whoever is sensitive as well as motor well knows this, and ought not to be ashamed of it. One who should pretend to be in *possession* of a *kraftige Seele*, would thereby prove himself a donkey ignorant of the conditions—the thing has to be conquered every moment afresh, by an act, and if writing and rhetoric help us to act, they are also part of the function and we need never be ashamed of them.

William James

How is one to restore savor to life when life has lost it? By making one's self able to play the piano well? By restoring one's self physically? By a gesture of the will? They are all absurd. All the same each one of us has (or probably has) his personal absurdity, by means of which to restore the status quo ante: the state in which one once enjoyed the mere act of being alive. To allow that act to become an act of misery or even, eventually, of terror is easy; to do the opposite is no less easy. You know what it is to be happy.

Wallace Stevens

Readers' Guide

It may be true that the author's revisions make it harder, not easier, for hurried readers; but flame kindles to the eye that contemplates it.

Marianne Moore

I'm all right [ ]. I take down not my Bible but Marcus Aurelius and follow up with Lucretius and Thoreau's Journal (The Heart of) and why couldn't somebody like Thoreau—a whole family of him—have ever settled here near me?

Lorine Niedecker

I'm really much more of a reader than a writer. I particularly like diaries . . . . I'm always reading in Thoreau's diaries, and my favorite book is the diaries of George Templeton Strong.

James Schuyler

The only poems I liked as a child were Paul Lawrence Dunbar's. And *Hiawatha*. But I liked any kind of stories. I read all of my mother's novels from the library: *The Rosary, The Mistress of Shenstone, Freckles, Edna Ferber,* all of Harold Bell Wright, and all of Zane Grey. I thought *Riders of the Purple Sage* a wonderful book and still think so, as I remember it.

Langston Hughes

I am glad there are Books.

They are better than Heaven for that is unavoidable while one may miss these.

Emily Dickinson

Right to Life

If Government knew how, I should like to see it check, not multiply, the population. When it reaches the true law of its action, every man that is born will be hailed as essential.

Ralph Waldo Emerson

If nobody had to die how would there be room enough for any of us who now live to have lived.

Gertrude Stein

I am saving a Miller for Mattie.

It laid six eggs on the Window Sill and I thought it was getting tired, so I killed it for her.

Emily Dickinson

Right to Privacy

Cannot we let people be themselves, and enjoy life in their own way? You are trying to make that man another *you*. One's enough.

Ralph Waldo Emerson

A private life is the long thick tree and the private life is the life for me. A tree which is thick is a tree which is thick. A life which is private is not what there is. All the times that come are the times I sing, all the singing I sing are the tunes I sing. I sing and I sing and the tunes I sing are what are tunes if they come and I sing. I sing I sing.

Gertrude Stein

The zoo shows us that privacy is a fundamental need of all animals.

Marianne Moore

Saving Grace

The artist can profitably forgo the scientific or philosophical attempt at grandeur and keep to what he knows, which is what everyone knows and does not dare accept, because he fears that knowledge is not reliable until it is explained, or rationalized, or proved; until, that is, it can be controlled by repetition like a scientific experiment. Art permits you to accept illogical immediacy, and in doing so releases you from chasing after the distant and the ideal. When this occurs, the effect is exalting.

Fairfield Porter

Experience in its immediacy seems perfectly fluent. The active sense of living which we all enjoy, before reflection shatters our instinctive world for us, is self-luminous and suggests no paradoxes. Its difficulties are disappointments and uncertainties. They are not intellectual contradictions.

When the reflective intellect gets at work, however, it discovers incomprehensibilities in the flowing process. Distinguishing its elements and parts, it gives them separate names, and what it thus disjoins it cannot easily put together. Pyrrhonism accepts the irrationality and revels in its dialectic elaboration. Other philosophies try, some by ignoring, some by resisting, and some by turning the dialectic procedure against itself, negating its first negations, to restore the fluent sense of life again, and let redemption take the place of innocence. The perfection with which any philosophy may do this is the measure of its human success and of its importance in philosophic history.

William James

School of Thought

Q: What is Transcendentalism, Mr. Emerson?
A: Well, why do you ask *me*?

Ralph Waldo Emerson

Secret Ingredient

The inadequacy of the work to the faculties, is the painful perception that keeps them still.

Ralph Waldo Emerson

Self-Portrait

As every man has his hobby-liking, mine is for a real farm-lane fenced by old chestnut-rails gray-green with dabs of moss and lichen, copious weeds and briers growing in spots athwart the heaps of stray-pick'd stones at the fence bases—irregular paths worn between, and horse and cow tracks—all characteristic accompaniments marking and scenting the neighborhood in their seasons—apple-tree blossoms in forward April—pigs, poultry, a field of August buckwheat, and in another the long flapping tassels of maize—and so to the pond, the expansion of the creek, the secluded-beautiful, with young and old trees, and such recesses and vistas.

Walt Whitman

Self-Reliance

No matter how complicated anything is, if it is not mixed up with remembering there is no confusion, but and that is the trouble with a great many so called intelligent people they mix up remembering with talking and listening, and as a result they have theories about anything but as remembering is repetition and confusion, and being existing that is listening and talking is action and not repetition intelligent people although they talk as if they knew something are really confusing, because they are so to speak keeping two times going at once, the repetition time of remembering and the actual time of talking but, and as they are rarely talking and listening, that is the talking being listening and the listening being talking, although they are clearly saying something they are not clearly creating something, because they are because they always are remembering, they are not at the same time talking and listening.

Gertrude Stein

Now as well as I can describe it, this characteristic attitude in me always involves an element of active tension, of holding my own, as it were, and trusting outward things to perform their part so as to make a full harmony, but without any *guaranty* that they will. Make it a guaranty—and the attitude immediately becomes to my consciousness stagnant and stingless. Take away the guaranty, and I feel (provided I am *überhaupt* in vigorous condition) a sort of deep enthusiastic bliss, of bitter willingness to do and suffer anything, which translates itself physically by a kind of stinging pain inside my breast-bone (don't smile at this—it is to me an essential element of the whole thing!), and which, although it is a mere mood or emotion to which I can give no form in words, authenticates itself to me as the deepest principle of all active and theoretic determination which I possess.

William James

It must often have occurred to Pollock that there was just a possibility that he wasn't an artist at all, that he had spent his life "toiling up the wrong road to art" as Flaubert said of Zola. But this very real possibility is paradoxically just what makes the tremendous excitement in his work. It is a gamble against terrific odds. Most reckless things are beautiful in some way, and recklessness is what makes experimental art beautiful, just as religions are beautiful because of the strong possibility that they are founded on nothing.

John Ashbery

Guile permits a lion to stalk a deer for food, or a Hitler to close in on a new country and therefore gain more food. But guile will never create a single book or a single picture or a single stained glass window that any human animal can contemplate with pride and say, "I, when not eating, made that."

Langston Hughes

Do not try to be saved—but let Redemption find you—as it certainly will—Love is it's own rescue, for we—at our supremest, are but it's trembling Emblems—

Emily Dickinson

There is something in my nature *furtive* like an old hen! You see a hen wandering up and down a hedgerow, looking apparently quite unconcerned, but presently she finds a concealed spot, and furtively lays an egg, and comes away as though nothing had happened. That is how I felt in writing *Leaves of Grass.*

Walt Whitman

The thing one gradually comes to find out is that one has no identity that is when one is in the act of doing anything. Identity is recognition, you know who you are because you and others remember anything about yourself but essentially you are not you when you are doing anything. I am I because my little dog knows me but creatively speaking the little dog knowing that you are you and your recognizing that he knows, that is what destroys creation. That is what makes school.

Gertrude Stein

But why I changed? Why I left the woods? I do not think that I can tell. I have often wished myself back there. I do not know any better how I ever came to go there. Perhaps it is none of my business, even if it is yours. Perhaps I wanted a change. There was a little stagnation, it may be. About 2 o'clock in the afternoon the world's axle creaked as if it needed greasing.

Henry David Thoreau

To summarize: Humility is an indispensable ally, enabling concentration to heighten gusto. There are always objectors, but we must not be too sensitive about not being liked or not being printed. David Low, the cartoonist, when carped at, said, "Ah, well—." But he has never compromised; he goes right on doing what idiosyncrasy tells him to do. The thing is to see the vision and not deny it; to care and admit that we do.

Marianne Moore

Sex to Sex

I sometimes remember we are to die, and hasten toward the Heart which how could I woo in a rendezvous where there is no Face?

Emily Dickinson

Why as I just look in the railroad car at some half turned face, do I love that woman? Though she is neither young nor fair complexioned?—She remains in my memory afterward for a year, and I calm myself to sleep at night by thinking of her.— Why be there men I meet, and others I know, that while they are with me, the sunlight of Paradise expands my blood—that when I walk with an arm of theirs around my neck, my soul scoots and courses like an unleashed dog—that when they leave me the pennants of my joy sink flat and lank in the deadest calm?—

Walt Whitman

From the necessity of loving none are exempt, and he that loves must utter his desires.

Ralph Waldo Emerson

Small Planet

This world is just a little place, just the red in the sky, before the sun rises, so let us keep fast hold of hands, that when the birds begin, none of us be missing.

Emily Dickinson

Society and Solitude

Why leave the place where life is—to go live with birds, bees, and caterpillars and bats? Life to me is where peoples is at— not just nature and snow and trees with falling leaves to rake

all by yourself, and furnaces to stoke, and no landlords down-
stairs to holler at to keep the heat up, and no next door
neighbors across the hall to raise a ruckus Saturday nights,
and no bad children drawing pictures on the walls in the halls,
and nobody to drink a beer with at the corner bar—because
the corner in the suburbans has nothing on it but a dim old
lonesome street light on a cold old lonesome pole.

Langston Hughes

I cannot get enough alone to write a letter to a friend. I
retreat & hide. I left the city, I hid myself in the pastures.
When I bought a house, the first thing I did was to plant trees.
I could not conceal myself enough. Set a hedge here, set pines
there, trees & trees, set evergreens, above all, for they will
keep my secret all the year round.

Ralph Waldo Emerson

I can't enter into social meetings . . . since I housekeep—
plural:houses—and write and read and walk and sew and sing
at the top of my voice when folky records are being played on
the phonograph.

Lorine Niedecker

There's nobody I'd rather meet; but life is only an inch long;
and a journey like that would destroy three days of it; and if
we should go to San Francisco we'd have to meet other people
and they would destroy other days. It is true without exaggera-
tion that I wouldn't drive over to Monterey to meet William
Shakespeare; this doesn't imply lack of admiration, or any-
thing more foolish than contentment at home.

Robinson Jeffers

Another ring at the door—enter Wm Dickinson—soon fol-
lowed by Mr Thurston! I again crept into the sitting room,
more dead than alive, and endeavored to *make conversation*.
Father looked round triumphantly. I remarked that "the
weather was rather cold" today, to which they all assented—
indeed I *never witnessed* such *wonderful unanimity*. Fled to my
mind again, and endeavored to procure something equally

agreeable with my *last happy remark*. Bethought me of Sabbath day, and the Rev. Mr Bliss, who preached upon it—remarked with wonderful emphasis, that I thought the Rev. gentleman a very remarkable preacher, and discovered a strong resemblance between himself & Whitfield, in the way of remark—I confess it *was rather* laughable, having never so much as seen the *ashes* of that gentleman*—but oh such a look as I got from my rheumatic sire. You should have seen it—I never can find language vivid eno' to portray it to you—well, pretty soon, another pull at the bell—enter *Thankful Smith*, in the furs and robes of her ancestors, while *James* brings up the rear.

Emily Dickinson

This spring I have had quite a number of invitations to come and talk here and there but I don't see the connection between writing poetry and delivering lectures. I am not a lecturer and I have no intention of doing that sort of thing except in cases in which I very much want to. It would be interesting to meet people in colleges, but then one never meets them at a lecture. If, for example, General Eisenhower should ask me to come down to Columbia and have a few highballs with him, that would be worth while. Yet it may be that, even if he did, when I got down there he would want to show me moving pictures of Hitler's funeral or something.

Wallace Stevens

Some are so inconsiderate as to ask to walk or sail with me, regularly every day—I have known such—and think that, because there will be six inches or a foot between our bodies, we shall not interfere! These things are settled by fate. The good ship sails—when she is ready. For freight or passage apply to—?? Ask my friend where. What is getting into a man's carriage when it is full, compared with putting your foot in his mouth and popping right into his mind without considering whether it is occupied or not? If I remember

---

*George Whitefield, the noted evangelist, had visited Jonathan Edwards at Northampton in 1740.

—Thomas H. Johnson, *The Letters of Emily Dickinson, Vol. I.*

aright, it was only on condition *that you were asked*, that you were to go with a man one mile or twain. Suppose a man asks, not you to go with him, but to go with you! Often I would rather undertake to shoulder a barrel of pork and carry it a mile than take into my company a man. It would not be so heavy a weight upon my mind. I could put it down and only feel my *back* ache for it.

Henry David Thoreau

Solitude is fearsome & heavy hearted. I have never known a man who had so much good accumulated upon him as I have. Reason, health, wife, child, friends, competence, reputation, the power to inspire. Yet leave me alone a few days, & I creep about as if in expectation of a calamity.

Ralph Waldo Emerson

Sensibility imposes silence which the imagination transmutes into eloquence and then, for the spiritual mariner, however northern, stranded, or chilled, there is society in solitude.

Marianne Moore

The Songs We Know Best

Women in These States approach the day of that organic equality with men, without which, I see, men cannot have organic equality among themselves. This empty dish, gallantry, will then be filled with something. This tepid wash, this diluted deferential love, as in songs, fictions, and so forth, is enough to make a man vomit; as to manly friendship, everywhere observed in The States, there is not the first breath of it to be observed in print. I say that the body of a man or woman, the main matter, is so far unexpressed in poems; but that the body is to be expressed, and sex is. . . . This is important in poems, because the whole of the other expressions of a nation are but flanges out of its great poems.

Walt Whitman

Ives is a great admirer of his old Yankee friend, Carl Ruggles, and his powerful music. At this concert, he sat quietly through the boos and jeers at his own music—but when that wonderful orchestral work, *Men and Mountains*, of Carl Ruggles was played, there were some hisses near him—and Ives jumped up and shouted You god damn sissy . . . when you hear strong masculine music like this, get up and use your ears like a man!

Charles Ives

Sons and Lovers

Be an opener of doors for such as come after thee, and do not try to make the universe a blind alley.

Ralph Waldo Emerson

Space Age

I said you see you look up and you see the cornice up there way on top clear in the air, but now in the new ones there is no cornice up there and that is right because why end anything, well anyway I always explained everything in America by this thing, the lack of passion that they call repression and gangsters, and savagery, and everybody being nice, and everybody not thinking because they had to drink and keep moving, in Europe when they drink they sit still but not in America no not in America and that is because there is no sky, there is no lid on top of them and so they move around or stand still and do not say anything. That makes that American language that says everything in two words and mostly in words of one syllable two words of one syllable and that makes all the conversation. That is the reason they like long books novels and things of a thousand pages it is to calm themselves from the need of two words and those words of one syllable that say everything.

Gertrude Stein

Light blue above, darker below, lightly roughened by the stir-
ring air and with smooth tracks on it. There goes Reynald
Hardy's lobster boat, taking a colorful load of pleasure-
seeking shoppers to Camden.
      O Air!

James Schuyler

I am always trying to tell this thing that a space of time is a
natural thing for an American to have always inside of them
as something in which they are continuously moving. Think
of anything, of cowboys, or movies, or detective stories, of
anybody who goes anywhere or stays at home and is an Ameri-
can and you will realize that it is something strictly American
to conceive a space that is filled with moving, a space of time
that is filled always filled with moving and my first real effort
to express this thing which is an American thing began in
writing The Making of Americans.

Gertrude Stein

Spin Control

Life defies our phrases, not only because it is infinitely continu-
ous and subtle and shaded, whilst our verbal terms are discrete,
rude and few; but because of a deeper discrepancy still. Our
words come together leaning on each other laterally for sup-
port, in chains and propositions, and there is never a proposi-
tion that does not require other propositions after it, to amplify
it, restrict it, or in some way save it from the falsity by defect or
excess which it contains. . . . Life, too, in one sense, stumbles
over its own fact in a similar way; for its earlier moments
plunge ceaselessly into later ones which reinterpret and correct
them. Yet there is something else than this in life, something
entirely unparalleled by anything in verbal thought. The living
moment—some living moments, at any rate—have somewhat
of absolute that needs no lateral support. Their meaning seems
to well up from out of their very centre, in a way impossible
verbally to describe. If you take a disk painted with a concentric

spiral pattern, and make it revolve, it will seem to be growing continuously and indefinitely, and yet to take in nothing from without; and to remain, if you pay attention to its actual size, always of the *same* size. Something as paradoxical as this lies in every present moment of life. Here or nowhere, as Emerson says, is the whole fact. The moment stands and contains and sums up all things; and all change is within it, much as the developing landscape with all its growth falls forever within the rear windowpane of the last car of a train that is speeding on its headlong way. This self-sustaining in the midst of self-removal, which characterizes all reality and fact, is something absolutely foreign to the nature of language, and even to the nature of logic, commonly so-called. Something forever far exceeds, escapes from statement, withdraws from definition, must be glimpsed and felt, not told.

William James

An attitude, physical or mental—a thought suggested by reading or in conversation—recurs with insistence. A few words coincident with the initial suggestion, suggest other words. Upon scrutiny, these words seem to have distorted the concept. The effort to effect a unit—in this case a poem—is perhaps abandoned. If the original, propelling sentiment reasserts itself with sufficient liveliness, a truer progress almost invariably accompanies it; and associated detail, adding impact to the concept, precipitates an acceptable development. To illustrate: a suit of armor is impressively poetic. The movable plates suggest the wearer; one is reminded of the armadillo and recalls the beauty of the ancient testudo. The idea of conflict, however, counteracts that of romance, and the subject is abandoned. However, the image lingers. Presently one encounters the iguana and is startled by the paradox of its docility in conjunction with its horrific aspect. The concept has been revived—of an armor in which beauty outweighs the thought of painful self-protectiveness. The emended theme compels development.

Marianne Moore

In the last few years I have been trying to keep meaningful-
ness up to the pace of randomness . . . but I really think that
meaningfulness can't get along without randomness and that
they somehow have to be brought together.

John Ashbery

A Star Is Born

When the success began and it was a success I got lost com-
pletely lost. You know the nursery rhyme, I am I because my
little dog knows me. Well you see I did not know myself, I lost
my personality. It has always been completely included in my-
self my personality as any personality naturally is, and here all
of a sudden, I was not just I because so many people did know
me. It was just the opposite of I am I because my little dog
knows me. So many people knowing me I was I no longer and
for the first time since I had begun to write I could not write
and what was worse I could not worry about not writing and
what was also worse I began to think about how my writing
would sound to others, how could I make them understand, I
who had always lived within myself and my writing.

Gertrude Stein

Supply Side

The merchants and company have long laughed at transcen-
dentalism, higher laws, &c., crying, "None of your moon-
shine," as if they were anchored to something not only defi-
nite, but sure and permanent. If there was any institution
which was presumed to rest on a solid and secure basis, and
more than any other represented this boasted common sense,
prudence, and practical talent, it was the bank; and now those
very banks are found to be mere reeds shaken by the wind.
Scarcely one in the land has kept its promise. It would seem as
if you only need live forty years in any age of this world, to see
its most promising government become the government of
Kansas, and banks nowhere. Not merely the Brook Farm and

Fourierite communities, but now the community generally has failed. But there is the moonshine still, serene, beneficent, and unchanged.

Henry David Thoreau

Talk Show

Of "shunning Men and Women"—they talk of Hallowed things, aloud—and embarrass my Dog—

Emily Dickinson

A Theory of Justice

As the greatest lessons of Nature throughout the universe are perhaps the lessons of variety and freedom, the same present the greatest lessons also in New World politics and progress.

Walt Whitman

One does not act rightly toward one's fellows if one does not know how to act rightly toward the earth.

Liberty Hyde Bailey

Things as They Are

The realist thinks he knows ahead of time what reality is, and the abstract artist what art is, but it is in its formality that realist art excels, and the best abstract art communicates an overwhelming sense of reality.

Fairfield Porter

You sometimes charge me with I know not what sky-blue, sky-void idealism. As far as it is a partiality, I fear I may be more deeply infected than you think me. I have very joyful dreams which I cannot bring to paper, much less to any approach to practice, and I blame myself not at all for my reveries, but that they have not yet got possession of my house and barn.

Ralph Waldo Emerson

Father called to say that our steelyard was fraudulent, exceeding by an ounce the rates of honest men. He had been selling oats. I cannot stop smiling, though it is hours since, that even our steelyard will not tell the truth.

Emily Dickinson

For nine readers out of ten, the necessary angel will appear to be the angel of the imagination and for nine days out of ten that is true, although it is the tenth day that counts.

Wallace Stevens

Thinking Like a Mountain

Man is made of the same atoms the world is, and shares the same impressions, predispositions, and destiny. When his mind is illuminated, when his heart is kind, he throws himself joyfully into the sublime order, and does, with knowledge, what the stones do by structure.

Ralph Waldo Emerson

We are parts in a living sensitive creation. The theme of evolution has overturned our attitude toward this creation. The living creation is not exclusively man-centered: it is biocentric. We perceive the essential community in nature, arising from within rather than from without, the forms of life proceeding upwardly and onwardly in something very like a mighty plan of sequence, man being one part in the process. We have genetic relation with all living things, and our aristocracy is the aristocracy of nature. We can claim no gross superiority and no isolated self-importance. The creation, and not man, is the norm.

Liberty Hyde Bailey

You must ascend a mountain to learn your relation to matter, and so to your own body, for *it* is at home there, though *you* are not. It might have been composed there, and will have no further to go to return to dust there, than in your garden; but your spirit inevitably comes away, and brings your body with it, if it lives. Just as awful really, and as glorious, is your garden. See how I can play with my fingers! They are the funniest companions I have ever found. Where did they come from? What strange control I have over them! *Who* am I? What are they?—those little peaks—call them Madison, Jefferson, Lafayette. What is *the matter? My* fingers ten, I say. Why, erelong, they may form the topmost crystal of Mount Washington. I go up there to see my body's cousins. There are some fingers, toes, bowels, &c., that I take an interest in, and therefore I am interested in all their relations.

Henry David Thoreau

We have looked first at man with his vanities and greed, and at his problems of a day or a year; and then only, and from this biased point of view, we have looked outward at the earth and at the universe of which our earth is so minute a part. Yet these are the great realities, and against them we see our human problems in a new perspective. Perhaps if we reversed the telescope and looked at man down these long vistas, we should find less time and inclination to plan for our own destruction.

Rachel Carson

Man is a part of nature, but a nearly infinitesimal part; the human race will cease after a while and leave no trace, but the great splendors of nature will go on. Meanwhile most of our time and energy are necessarily spent on human affairs; that can't be prevented though I think it can be minimized; but for philosophy, which is an endless research of truth, and for contemplation, which can be a sort of worship, I would suggest that the immense beauty of the earth and the outer universe, the divine "nature of things," is a more rewarding object. Certainly it is more ennobling. It is a source of strength; the other of distraction.

Robinson Jeffers

For myself, the indefinite, the impersonal, atmospheres and oceans and, above all, the principle of order are precisely what I love; and I dont see why, for a philosopher, they should not be the ultimate inamorata.

Wallace Stevens

Man would be better, more sane and more happy, if he devoted less attention and less passion (love, hate, etc.) to his own species, and more to non-human nature. Extreme introversion in any single person is a kind of insanity; so it is in a race; and race has always and increasingly spent too much thought on itself and too little on the world outside.

Robinson Jeffers

The journey of the rock is never ended. In every tiny part of any living thing are materials that once were rock that turned to soil. . . .

So—here we go. Maybe as rocks and I pass each other I could say how-do-you-do to an agate.

Lorine Niedecker

This Land Is Your Land

California is sown thick with the names of all the big and little saints. Chase them away and substitute aboriginal names. What is the fitness—What the strange charm of aboriginal names?—Monongahela—it rolls with venison richness upon the palate. Among names to be revolutionized: that of the city of "Baltimore."

Walt Whitman

I think the American Revolution bought its glory cheap. If the problem was new, it was simple. If there were few people, they were united, and the enemy 3,000 miles off. But now, vast property, gigantic interests, family connections, webs of party, cover the land with a network that immensely multiplies the dangers of war.

Ralph Waldo Emerson

The things that used to be the romantic thing indians and cow boys and those things to any American are not really now romantic things. And to any American in coming back to America other things are not romantic any more, gangsters or speak easies, the thing that has come to be the romantic thing for an American coming back to America and wandering are the ordinary ways of living the ways that the states and the cities have come to have as their natural thing, it is that that is the romantic thing to an American coming back to America. The fact that they all talk American, that strikes one as it does the American going to France that they all talk French. Then the simple things they do which have come to be in the every day living and writing of the country when the returned American sees that the every day things they do it is that that makes him feel romantic and then there is the particular thing. When you see the home town of a manufactured thing and the place they make it being so simply where it belongs like the Champion spark plugs in Toledo the McCormick farm implements in Chicago not to mention the Ford car being at home in Detroit Michigan all that makes you feel it is strange and real and there and therefore romantic and when you pass Marion Ohio unexpectedly and you know the book Mr. Harding or Wilbur Wright's picture field or are taken out to Edison's studio it is that that makes you feel that it is natural and strange and there and therefore romantic and not at all as you had expected although exactly as you have been told.

Gertrude Stein

I looked out the window of the Pullman at the great muddy river flowing down toward the heart of the South, and I began to think what that river, the old Mississippi, had meant to Negroes in the past—how to be sold down the river was the worst fate that could overtake a slave in times of bondage. Then I remembered reading how Abraham Lincoln had made a trip down the Mississippi on a raft to New Orleans, and how he had seen slavery at its worst, and had decided within himself that it should be removed from American life. Then I began to think about other rivers in our past—the Congo, and the Niger, and the Nile in Africa—and the thought came to me: "I've known rivers," and I put it down on the back of an envelope I had in my pocket, and within the space of ten or fifteen minutes, as the train gathered speed in the dusk, I had written this poem, which I called "The Negro Speaks of Rivers."

Langston Hughes

My own country never interested me very much either, and I didn't read very much American literature or think that there could be much value in doing so. I was sort of a snob about it as I was growing up. Everything around me seemed dull and pedestrian, and I was always imagining that things were more interesting in Europe or somewhere else.

John Ashbery

Here in Hartford is an exhibition of an American landscapist of a century ago: Thomas Cole. This man gives one something. But he also shocks one's dreams. For all that, I like to hold on to anything that seems to have a definite American past even though the American trees may be growing by the side of queer Parthenons set, say, in the neighborhood of Niagara Falls. One is so homeless over here in such things and something really American is like meeting a beautiful cousin or, for that matter, even one's mother for the first time.

Wallace Stevens

Tradition and the Individual Talent

When the student leader of a prayer meeting into which I had wandered casually to look local religion over, suddenly and without warning announced that "Professor Du Bois would lead us in prayer," I simply answered "No, he won't," and as a result nearly lost my job.

W. E. B. Du Bois

When a Child and fleeing from Sacrament I could hear the
Clergyman saying "All who loved the Lord Jesus Christ—
were asked to remain—"

My flight kept time to the Words.

Emily Dickinson

Twenty-First Century

What are they going to try next, what does the twenty-first
century want to do about it? They certainly will not want to be
organized, the twentieth century is seeing the end of that,
perhaps as the virgin lands will by that time be pretty well
used up, and also by that time everybody will have been as
quickly everywhere as anybody can be, perhaps they will be-
gin looking for liberty again and individually amusing them-
selves again and old-fashioned or dirt farming.

Gertrude Stein

Well in a kind of way the American of the pre-Civil War
and the Civil War Americans who listened to Lincoln, they
were more interesting than the Roosevelt to Roosevelt
American, and now I am completely and entirely sure that
we are going to be more interesting again, be a sad and
quiet people who can listen and who can promise and who
can perform.

Gertrude Stein

Uncertainty Principle

Life is in the transitions as much as in the terms connected;
often, indeed, it seems to be there the more emphatically, as if
our spurts and sallies forward were the real firing-line of the
battle, were like the thin line of flame advancing across the
dry autumnal field which the farmer proceeds to burn.

William James

Every thing teaches transition, transference, metamorphosis:
therein is human power, in transference, not in creation; &
therein is human destiny, not in longevity, but in removal. We
dive & reappear in new places.

Ralph Waldo Emerson

Vanity Fair

We are suffering from too much sarcasm, I feel. Any touch of
unfeigned gusto in our smart press is accompanied by an arch
word implying, "Now to me, of course, this is a bit asinine."
Denigration, indeed, is to me so disaffecting that when I was
asked to write something for the Columbia Chapter of Phi
Beta Kappa Class Day exercises, I felt that I should not let my
sense of incapacity as an orator hinder me from saying what I
feel about the mildew of disrespect and leave appreciation to
Mr. Auden, to salute "literary marines landing in little maga-
zines." I then realized that what I was so urgent to emphasize
is reduced in the First Psalm to a sentence: Blessed is the man
who does not sit in the seat of the scoffer.

Marianne Moore

Vote with Your Feet

I found Henry T. yesterday in my woods. He thought nothing
to be hoped from you, if this bit of mould under your feet was
not sweeter to you to eat, than any other in this world, or in
any world.

Ralph Waldo Emerson

War and Peace

In a World too full of Beauty for Peace, I have met nothing
more beautiful.

Emily Dickinson

The Weather

Hard clouds, & hard expressions, & hard manners, I love.

Ralph Waldo Emerson

As for me, I love screaming, wrestling, boiling-hot days.

Walt Whitman

Wild Blue Yonder

I always liked boats but rocked in the cradle of the deep is nothing to being rocked in the cradle of the sky, the air is so sweetly solid and being able to go every way is so much better than just being able to go one way. The earth now, as far as I am concerned, is something that has been, and when you come back to it, it is a disappointment and the other side of the clouds is all right, you know that by its light, the light of the clouds, the white light of the clouds, and you recognize it, but you like it more than just recognizing.

Gertrude Stein

What is so good in a college as an observatory? The sublime attaches to the door & to the first stair you ascend, that this is the road to the stars. Every fixture & instrument in the building, every nail & pin has a direct reference to the Milky-Way, the fixed stars, & the nebulae. & we leave Massachusetts & the Americas & history outside at the door, when we came in.

Ralph Waldo Emerson

Nothing too close, nothing too far off . . . the stars not too far off.

Walt Whitman

Sources

Preface

Love is the bright foreigner, ...
> Ralph Waldo Emerson, "Aug 29? 1849," *Emerson in His Journals,* Joel Porte ed. (Cambridge: Harvard/Belknap, 1982), 404.

Anxiety of Influence

The United States is just now . . . .
> Gertrude Stein, "Why I Do Not Live in America," *How Writing Is Written,* Robert Bartlett Haas ed. (Los Angeles: Black Sparrow Press, 1974), 51.

As an adolescent, the thing I most seriously wanted . . . .
> James Schuyler, "Schuyler in Conversation," Raymond Foye int., *XXIst Century,* I, no. 1 (Winter 1991/1992), 46.

It was like throwing . . . .
> Langston Hughes, *The Big Sea* (New York: Alfred A. Knopf, 1940), 98. Quoted in Arnold Rampersad, *The Life of Langston Hughes, Vol. I, 1902–1941: I, Too, Sing America* (New York: Oxford University Press, 1986), 72.

Now, when all the primitive difficulties . . . .
> Wallace Stevens, "Connecticut," *Opus Posthumous* (New York: Alfred A. Knopf, 1957), 295.

One book only did Hughes save. . . .
> Rampersad, *Life of Langston Hughes, Vol. I,* 72.

I had no intention . . . . .
> Hughes, "The Big Sea," draft ms. Quoted in Rampersad, *Life of Langston Hughes, Vol. I,* 72.

The Art of Losing*

To be worthy of what we lose . . . .

> Emily Dickinson, "To T. W. Higginson, summer 1882," *The Letters of Emily Dickinson, Vol. III*, Thomas H. Johnson ed. (Cambridge: Harvard/Belknap, 1958), 737.

As Big as You Please

And also, from hence gather . . . .

> John Cotton, "Limitation of Government," in *The American Puritans*, Perry Miller ed. (Garden City, N.Y.: Doubleday/Anchor, 1956), 87–88.

My wickedness, as I am in myself, . . .

> Jonathan Edwards, "Personal Narrative," *The Norton Anthology of American Literature, Vol. I* (New York: W.W. Norton, 1979), 217–18.

In all my lectures, I have taught . . . .

> Emerson, "Apr 7? 1840," *Emerson in His Journals*, 236.

Being a Genius

It is not possible to prepare . . . .

> Marianne Moore, "If a Man Die," *The Complete Prose of Marianne Moore*, Patricia C. Willis ed. (New York: Viking, 1986), 285.

It takes a lot of time to be a genius, . . .

> Stein, *Everybody's Autobiography* (New York: Vintage, 1973), 70.

Look sharply after your thoughts. . . .

> Emerson, "Oct 1872," *The Heart of Emerson's Journals*, Bliss Perry ed. (Cambridge: Houghton Mifflin/The Riverside Press, 1926), 333.

One never knows . . . .

> John Ashbery, "Craft Interview with John Ashbery," William Packard int., *The Craft of Poetry* (Garden City, N.Y.: Doubleday, 1974), 118.

The neologisms of talk . . . .

> Stevens, "To Thomas McGreevy, Oct 7 1948," *Letters of Wallace Stevens*, Holly Stevens ed. (New York: Knopf, 1966), 618.

---

*Were Departure Separation, there would be neither Nature nor Art, for there would be no World—
—Emily Dickinson, "Prose Fragment 52," *Letters, Vol. III*, 920.

Results should not be too voluntarily aimed at . . . .
>William James, *The Letters of William James, Vol. I* (New York: Longmans, 1920), 133. Quoted in Jacques Barzun, *A Stroll with William James* (New York: Harper & Row, 1983), 107.

Q: Did you awake to it, . . .
>Hughes, "Chatting with Langston Hughes," Linwood Stevens int., *Morehouse College Maroon Tiger* (January–February, 1947), 17–18. Quoted in Arnold Rampersad, *The Life of Langston Hughes, Vol. II, 1947–1967: I Dream a World* (New York: Oxford University Press, 1988), 129.

The Body Electric

It occurred to me when I awoke . . . .
>Henry David Thoreau, "Sep 12 1853," *Selected Journals*, Carl Bode ed. (New York: Signet/New American Library, 1967), 189.

I am glad if Theodore . . . .
>Dickinson, "To Mrs. J. G. Holland, early Jun 1884," *Letters, Vol. III*, 824.

Captivity Narrative

Our philosophy is to *wait*. . . .
>Emerson, "Oct 1848," *Emerson in His Journals*, 394.

The Common Defense

Hitler and Germany can be smashed . . . .
>Robinson Jeffers, "To Herbert Carlin," *The Selected Letters of Robinson Jeffers*, Ann N. Ridgeway ed. (Baltimore: Johns Hopkins, 1968), 226n.

Has the Mexican war terminated . . . .
>Dickinson, "To Austin Dickinson, Oct 21 1847," *The Letters of Emily Dickinson, Vol. I*, Thomas H. Johnson ed. (Cambridge: Harvard/Belknap, 1958), 49.

The whole present system . . . .
>Walt Whitman, "Democratic Vistas," *Complete Poetry and Collected Prose* (New York: The Library of America, 1982), 956n.

That evening I went over to talk . . . .
>Stein, "Off We All Went to See Germany," *Life* (August 6, 1945) 54–58. Quoted in *Gertrude Stein's America*, Gilbert A. Harrison ed. (New York: Liveright, 1965), 42–43.

There can be no thought of escape. . . .
>Stevens, "The Irrational Element in Poetry," *Opus Posthumous* (1957), 224–25.

Communion of Saints

We cannot wonder at the aversion . . . .
> Margaret Fuller, "The Great Lawsuit," *The Norton Anthology of American Literature, Vol. I,* 1414.

Many will say it is a dream, . . .
> Whitman, "Democratic Vistas," *Poetry and Prose* (Library of America), 982n.

The loveliest sermon . . . .
> Dickinson, "To Frances Norcross, early 1873," *The Letters of Emily Dickinson, Vol. II,* Thomas H. Johnson ed. (Cambridge: Harvard/Belknap, 1958), 502–3.

Saints II

Do we not already sing our love . . . .
> Aldo Leopold, "The Land Ethic," *A Sand County Almanac, and Sketches Here and There* (New York: Oxford University Press, 1987), 204.

The Conduct of Life

Does Wisdom work in a tread-mill? . . .
> Thoreau, "Life without Principle," *Thoreau's Vision: The Major Essays,* Charles R. Anderson ed. (Englewood Cliffs, N.J.: Prentice-Hall, 1973), 181.

Consent of the Governed

I don't envisage collectivism. . . .
> Stein, "Answer to Eugene Jolas," *How Writing Is Written,* 53.

Not a man faces round . . . .
> Whitman, "Letter to Ralph Waldo Emerson (Appendix to *Leaves of Grass,* 1856)," *Poetry and Prose* (Library of America), 1331.

The Leaves are flying high away, . . .
> Dickinson, "To Mrs. J. G. Holland, late autumn 1884," *Letters, Vol. III,* 849.

The Creation

We live in a scientific age; . . .
> Rachel Carson, "National Book Award Acceptance Speech, 1953," in Paul Brooks, *The House of Life: Rachel Carson at Work* (Boston: Houghton Mifflin, 1972), 128.

If we knew more chemistry and physics . . . .
> Lorine Niedecker, "To Louis Zukofsky, Apr 29 1945," in " 'Knee

Deck Her Daisies:' Selections from her Letters to Louis Zukofsky," Jenny Penberthy ed., *Sulfur* 18 (Winter 1987), 112. Also in Jenny Penberthy, *Niedecker and the Correspondence with Zukofsky, 1931–1970* (New York: Cambridge University Press, 1993), 134–35.

Science will not trust us . . . .

Dickinson, "To Mrs. J. G. Holland, about Sep 1873," *Letters, Vol. II,* 511.

Credits

No other American colonial author . . . .

Thomas Jefferson, quoted in *Congregational Church and Parish, Essex, Mass.* (Essex: Essex Congregational Church, 1933), 31. Quoted again in Junior League of Boston, *Along the Coast of Essex County* (Amesbury, Mass.: Essex County Tourist Council, 1975), 140.

Few bodies or parties have served the world so well . . . .

Emerson, "Jan 1824," *Emerson in His Journals,* 39.

I was simmering, simmering, simmering; . . .

Whitman, quoted in John Townsend Trowbridge, *My Story: With Recollections of Noted Persons* (Boston: Houghton Mifflin, 1903), 366–67. Quoted again in Gay Wilson Allen, *Walt Whitman Handbook* (New York: Hendricks House, 1962), 30.

The reading of the divine Emerson, . . .

James, "To Henry James," *The Letters of William James, Vol. II* (New York: Longmans, 1920), 190. Quoted in F. O. Matthiessen, *The James Family* (New York: Knopf, 1947), 431.

With the Kingdom of Heaven on his knee, . . .

Dickinson, "To T. W. Higginson, about Oct 1870," *Letters, Vol. II,* 482. Also in Richard B. Sewall, *The Life of Emily Dickinson, Vol. II* (New York: Farrar Straus & Giroux, 1974), 570.

Margaret Fuller talking of Women, said, . . .

Emerson, "Oct 20 1837," *Emerson in His Journals,* 172.

As for taking T.'s arm, . . .

Emerson, "Jul–Aug 1848," *Emerson in His Journals,* 391.

Dramatic unities; laws of versification; . . .

James, "To George H. Palmer, Apr 2 1900," *The Selected Letters of William James,* Elizabeth Hardwick ed. (Boston: Godine/Nonpareil, 1980), 183.

One resents the cavil . . . .

Moore, "Emily Dickinson," *The Complete Prose,* 291.

No matter how often what happened had happened . . . .

    Stein, "Portraits and Repetitions," *Lectures in America*, Wendy Steiner ed. (Boston: Beacon Press, 1985), 169.

Eventually it [philosophy] landed me squarely in the arms of . . . .

    W. E. B. Du Bois, *Dusk of Dawn: An Essay Toward an Autobiography of a Race Concept*, in *Writings* (New York: Library of America, 1986), 578. Du Bois, *Dusk of Dawn* (New York: Harcourt Brace, 1940), 33.

A vaporous and cryptic prose style . . . .

    Donald Worster ed., *American Environmentalism: The Formative Period, 1860–1915* (New York: John Wiley, 1973), 223.

My earliest memories of written words . . . .

    Hughes, *Freedomways* (1st Quarter 1965), 11. Quoted in *Life of Langston Hughes, Vol. I*, 19.

Again we are reminded that the twentieth century, . . .

    Ashbery, "Gertrude Stein," *Reported Sightings: Art Chronicles, 1957–1987*, David Bergman ed. (New York: Alfred A. Knopf, 1989), 107.

I do know that I don't know how to account . . . .

    Moore, "Foreword to *A Marianne Moore Reader*," *The Complete Prose*, 552.

Refusal to speak . . . .

    Moore, "Conjuries that Endure," *The Complete Prose*, 349.

Dear fat Stevens, . . .

    William Carlos Williams, "Prologue to *Kora in Hell*," *Imaginations* (New York: New Directions, 1970), 27.

The pure products of America don't always go crazy. . . .

    Ashbery, "In the American Grain," *The New York Review of Books*, XX, no. 2 (February 22, 1973), 3–6.

We all strive for safety, . . .

    Leopold, quoted in Roderick Frazier Nash, *The Rights of Nature* (Madison: University of Wisconsin, 1989), 63.

All the mud of mankind's . . . .

    Hughes, "Jeffers: Man, Sea, and Poetry," *Carmel Pine Cone*, Jan 10, 1941. Quoted in *Life of Langston Hughes, Vol. I*, 393.

When you think of what her life might be . . . .

    Stevens, "To Barbara Church, Apr 9 1951," *Letters*, 715.

I consider her the most famous Negro woman poet . . . .

    Hughes, *New York Times*, Apr 14 1967. Quoted in *Life of Langston Hughes, Vol. II*, 419–20.

Inimitable, irresistible Langston, . . .

    Moore, "To Langston Hughes, Dec 30 1966." Quoted in *Life of Langston Hughes, Vol. I*, 3.

I'd known her about two years, ...

> Gail Roub, comments at "Remembering Lorine Niedecker," on the occasion of her posthumous receipt of the Banta Award, Wisconsin Library Association, October, 1986.

I would work most of each night ....

> Carson, in Brooks, *The House of Life: Rachel Carson at Work*, 5.

He painted his surroundings ....

> Ashbery, "Fairfield Porter," *Reported Sightings*, 317.

Sometimes I hear him typing, ...

> Fairfield Porter, "To Frank O'Hara, Aug 1 1955," quoted in John T. Spike, *Fairfield Porter: An American Classic* (New York: Harry N. Abrams, 1992), 120.

Q: "Do you see any new trends? ...

> Schuyler, interview, *Contemporary Authors*, Vol. 101, 447.

Also Appearing

For England's sake they are going from England, ...

> Edward Johnson, "Wonder-Working Providence of Sion's Savior," *The American Puritans*, 35.

Mr. Cotton pronounced the sentence of admonition ....

> John Winthrop, "Mar 1 1638," Journal, in *The American Puritans*, 58.

Decoration Day

I noticed that Robert Browning ....

> Dickinson, "To Louise and Frances Norcross, 1864?" *Letters, Vol. II*, 436.

Dedication

I write for myself and strangers, ...*

> Stein, "The Gradual Making of *The Making of Americans*," *Lectures in America*, 141, quoting *The Making of Americans* (New York: Harcourt, Brace and Company, 1934), 211.

---

*Very often people don't listen to you when you speak to them. It's only when you talk to yourself that they prick up their ears.
—John Ashbery, quoted in David Lehman, "The Pleasures of John Ashbery's Poetry," *The Line Forms Here* (Ann Arbor: The University of Michigan Press, 1992), 168.

Happy is he who looks only . . . .
  Emerson, "Mar–Apr 1848," *Emerson in His Journals*, 384.

Democratic Vistas

The end of all good government . . . .
  John Wise, "Vindication of the Government of New England Churches," in *The American Puritans*, 136–37.
Man's external, personal, natural liberty, . . .
  Wise, "Vindication," in *The American Puritans*, 127–28.
The important thing . . . .
  Stein, *The Autobiography of Alice B. Toklas*, in *Selected Writings of Gertrude Stein*, Carl Van Vechten ed. (New York: Random House, 1946), 145.

The Discovery of America

Linnaeus said long ago, . . .
  Thoreau, "The Wild," *Thoreau's Vision: The Major Essays*, Charles R. Anderson ed. (Englewood Cliffs, N.J.: Prentice-Hall, 1973), 142–43.
One turns with something like ferocity . . . .
  Stevens, "John Crowe Ransom: Tennessean," *Opus Posthumous* (revised edition), Milton J. Bates ed. (New York: Alfred A. Knopf, 1989), 248.
I have become a vegetable, . . .
  James, "To Frances R. Morse, Apr 30 1901," quoted in Ralph Barton Perry, *The Thought and Character of William James: Briefer Version* (New York: George Braziller, 1954), 256.

Doing Your Thing

Our forefathers walked . . . .
  Emerson, "Aug 1841," *Emerson in His Journals*, 258.
It is awfully important to know . . . .
  Stein, "What Is English Literature," *Lectures in America*, 13–14.
Life is a selection, . . .
  Emerson, "May–Jun 1846," *Emerson in His Journals*, 357.
After the early period of absorbing influences. . . .
  Ashbery, "Jane Freilicher," *Reported Sightings*, 241.
Do your thing . . . .
  Emerson, "Jul 7 1839," *Emerson in His Journals*, 221.

Lost in Translation*

Some of the young people . . .

> George Bush, in Maureen Dowd, "Bush Boasts of Turnaround from 'Easy Rider' Society," *New York Times,* October 7, 1988, B7.

I've gotten over . . . .

> George Bush, in Maureen Dowd, "For Bush on the Campaign Trail, The Style Is First Sour, Then Sweet," *New York Times,* October 12, 1988, A24.

---

*Sam Patch's slogan became, according to the W.P.A. Guide, *Rochester and Monroe County* (Rochester, N.Y.: Scrantom's, 1937, p. 93), a "catch-phrase" of its times: "For years it was a slang expression, not only locally but nationally." Emerson was twenty-six when Patch leaped to his death on November 13, 1829. The sentence, "Do your thing & I shall know you," appears in Emerson's *Journals* for July 7, 1839, and again in "Self-Reliance" as published in his *Essays* of 1841.

Do something, it matters little or not at all whether it be in the way of what you call your profession or not, so it be in the plane or coincident with the axis of your character. Strike the hardest blow you can, & always do this by work which is agreeable to your nature. This is economy.
—Ralph Waldo Emerson, "Nov 13 1839 *[Journals]*," *Selected Writings of Ralph Waldo Emerson,* William H. Gilman ed. (New York: Signet/New American Library, 1965), 86–87.

Do what you love. Know your own bone: gnaw at it, bury it, unearth it, and gnaw still. Do not be too moral. You may cheat yourself out of much life so. Aim above morality. Be not simply good; be good for something.
—Henry David Thoreau, "To Harrion Gray Otis Blake, Mar 27 1848," *Letters to Various Persons,* Ralph Waldo Emerson ed. (Boston: James R. Osgood and Company, 1877), 46. Reprinted in facsimile (Cambridge: Folcroft Library Editions, 1971), 46.

Went to-day to see this just finished painting by John Mulvaney. . . . I advised him if it went abroad to take it to Paris. I think they might appreciate it there—nay, they certainly would. Then I would like to show Monsieur Crapeau that some things can be done in America as well as others.
—Walt Whitman, "Custer's Last Rally [Aug 1881]," *Specimen Days* (Boston: David R. Godine, 1971), 114–15.

Do your own thing. Don't be afraid . . . .

> Nancy Reagan, in Michael Wines, "First Lady Hopes for Unglamorous Legacy," *New York Times*, January 15, 1989, 20.

The doctrine of do your own thing, . . .

> William J. Bennett, Conservative Leadership Conference, AIM, *C-Span*, December 1, 1989.

You always get ups and downs. . . .

> Barbara Bush, in "From Pit Bull to President," *Newsweek*, November 12, 1990, 30.

Some things can be done as well as others.

> Sam Patch, in Henry W. Clune, *The Genesee* (New York: Holt, Rinehart and Winston, 1963), 238.

Droll Yankee

Am I the American indeed— . . .

> Niedecker, "To Cid Corman, Dec 15 1966," quoted in Cid Corman, "With Lorine," *At Their Word: Essays on the Arts of Language, Vol. II* (Santa Barbara: Black Sparrow, 1978), 191.

I saw two Bushes fight just now— . . .

> Dickinson, "Prose Fragment 82," *Letters, Vol. III*, 924.

Dying Words

Moose. Indian.

> Thoreau, "A Detailed Chronology of Thoreau's Life," *The Annotated Walden*, Philip Van Doren Stern ed. (New York: Clarkson Potter, 1970), 136.

Each and All

I need hardly say . . . .

> Emerson, "Nov 14, 1839," *Emerson in His Journals*, 230.

Economy

I am glad you love the Blossoms . . . .

> Dickinson, "To Eugenia Hall, early 1876," *Letters, Vol. II*, 550.

Effects of Analogy

There is something endearing . . . .

> Schuyler, "Aug 20 1969," *For Joe Brainard* (New York: Dia Art Foundation, Readings in Contemporary Poetry No. 9, 1988), 25. Also in Schuyler, *The Home Book*, Trevor Winkfield ed. (Calais, Vt.: Z Press, 1977), 93.

The other day at last I saw . . . .

> Schuyler, "Jul 21 1969," *For Joe Brainard*, 18.

Empowerment

It would be a pity to dissolve the union . . . .
> Emerson, "Jan–Mar 1844," *Emerson in His Journals*, 323.

The End of Beauty

It will probably be centuries, . . .
> Charles Ives, "Some Quarter-Tone Impressions," *Essays Before a Sonata, The Majority, and Other Writings,* Howard Boatwright ed. (New York: W. W. Norton, 1970), 109.

There are beauties that are more palpable . . . .
> Edwards, "Images and Shadows of Divine Things," *The Norton Anthology of American Literature, Vol. I,* 260.

I think ten million supple-wristed gods . . . .
> Whitman, "Other Notebooks, &c. on Words," *Daybooks and Notebooks, Vol. III: Diary in Canada, Notebooks, Index,* William White ed., in *The Collected Writings of Walt Whitman* (New York: New York University Press, 1977), 770.

The processes of art, . . .
> Williams, "Preface," *Selected Essays* (New York: New Directions, 1969), n.p.

The End of History

To the Twentieth Century . . . .
> Stein, "How Writing Is Written," *How Writing Is Written,* 157.

This as I say has been the great problem . . . .
> Stein, "Portraits and Repetition," *Lectures in America,* 190–91.

On the other hand, perhaps these . . . .
> Ashbery, "The Invisible Avant-Garde," *Reported Sightings,* 393.

End of Ideology

What are philosophers, scientists, . . .
> Williams, "The Work of Gertrude Stein," *Imaginations,* 347–48.

Epigraph

Perchance, when, in the course of ages, . . .
> Thoreau, "The Wild," *Thoreau's Vision: The Major Essays,* 149. Also Thoreau, "Walking," *The American Transcendentalists,* Perry Miller ed. (Garden City, N.Y.: Doubleday/Anchor, 1957), 148. Thoreau's own title was "Walking, or The Wild."

E Pluribus Unum*

We Americans have yet to really learn . . . .
  Whitman, "The Spanish Element in Our Nationality," *November Boughs,* in *Poetry and Prose* (Library of America), 1146.
Manistique, Indian name for vermillion . . . .
  Niedecker, "Lake Superior Country: vacation trip '66" (unpublished ms. notes, 1966), 3. Quoted in part in my article, "On Lorine Niedecker," *Raritan,* XII, no. 2 (Fall 1992), 65. By permission of Cid Corman, Literary Executor for the Estate of Lorine Niedecker.
As to that composite American identity . . . .
  Whitman, "The Spanish Element in Our Nationality," *Poetry and Prose* (Library of America), 1147.

Equal Protection

And in this country one sees . . . .
  Emerson, "The Fugitive Slave Law," *The Works of Ralph Waldo Emerson, Vol. XI: Miscellanies* (Boston: Houghton Mifflin/The Riverside Press, 1883), 213.

Errand into the Wilderness

There is another combination. . . .
  Cotton, quoted by Perry Miller ed., in *The American Puritans,* 171.
The "ability to be drunk with a sudden realization . . . .
  Moore, "Things Others Never Notice," *The Complete Prose,* 327.

Native Americans. I hate the narrowness of the native American party. . . . Man is the most composite of all creatures, the wheel insect, *volvox globator,* is at the beginning. Well, as in the burning of the Temple at Corinth, by the melting & intermixture of silver & gold & other metals, a new compound more precious than any, called the Corinthian Brass, was formed, so in this Continent,—asylum of all nations, the energy of Irish, Germans, Swedes, Poles, & Cossacks, & all the European tribes,—of the Africans, & of the Polynesians, will construct a new race, a new religion, a new State, a new literature, which will be as vigorous as the new Europe which came out of the smelting pot of the Dark Ages, or that which emerged earlier from the Pelasgic & Etruscan barbarism.
—Ralph Waldo Emerson, "Sep–Oct 1845," *Selected Writings of Ralph Waldo Emerson,* William H. Gilman ed. (New York: Signet/New American Library, 1965), 128.

Talk of mysteries! . . .

> Thoreau, "Climbing Mt. Ktaadn," *Thoreau's Vision*, 118–19.

Now, here lies a difficulty . . . .

> Liberty Hyde Bailey, *The Holy Earth* (New York: Charles Scribner's Sons, 1915), 23–24. Reprinted as Bailey, *The Holy Earth* (Ithaca, N.Y.: Comstock Publishing Co., 1919), 23–24.

He will have the earth receive . . . .

> Whitman, "Walt Whitman and His Poems" [anonymous 1855 review of his own work], in Sam Abrams ed., *The Neglected Walt Whitman: Vital Texts* (New York: Four Walls Eight Windows, 1993), 134–35.

Oh Matchless Earth— . . .

> Dickinson, "To Susan Gilbert Dickinson, about 1870," *Letters, Vol. II*, 478.

Expanding Universe

I live a good while & acquire . . . .

> Emerson, "Jul 1852," *Emerson in His Journals*, 436.

Fame*

Do you see what I mean when I say anybody . . . .

> Stein, "American Crimes and How They Matter," *How Writing Is Written*, 104.

Fashion

Whatever the cut, width, or foot, . . .

> Moore, "Dress and Kindred Subjects," *The Complete Prose*, 596.

Fate of the Earth

Life is a spell so exquisite . . . .

> Dickinson, "To Louise and Frances Norcross, late Apr 1873," *Letters, Vol. II*, 506.

---

*How stern a moral may be drawn from the story of poor Sam Patch. Why do we call him a madman or a fool when he has left his memory around the falls of the Genesee more permanent than if the letters of his name had been hewn into the forehead of the precipice? Was the leaper of cataracts more mad or foolish than other men who throw away life, or misspend it in pursuit of empty fame, and seldom so triumphantly as he?
—Nathaniel Hawthorne, quoted in Clune, *The Genesee*, 242.

Some of the thoughts that came . . . .
> Carson, "To Ruth Nanda Anschen, Jan 30 1958," in Brooks, *The House of Life,* 9–10.

Torrential rains, water rising . . . .
> Niedecker, *"Between Your House and Mine:" The Letters of Lorine Niedecker to Cid Corman, 1960 to 1970,* Lisa Pater Faranda ed. (Durham, N.C.: Duke University Press, 1986), 71.

Foreign Affairs

I was much taken with what one American soldier said . . . .
> Stein, *Wars I Have Seen* (New York: Random House, 1945), 258–59.

And for Americans who feel . . . .
> Ashbery, "In the American Grain," *The New York Review of Books,* Feb 22 1973, 6.

Form Follows Function

Let a brave, devout man . . . .
> Thoreau, "A Winter Walk," *Thoreau's Vision,* 44.

You spoke of "Hope" surpassing "Home"— . . .
> Dickinson, "To Otis P. Lord, about 1879," *Letters, Vol. II,* 638.

Even as a boy, I had the fancy, . . .
> Whitman, "Seashore Fancies," *Specimen Days* (Boston: David R. Godine, 1971), 67. Also in *Poetry and Prose* (Library of America), 796–97.

Founding Fathers

We, John Wise, John Andrews, . . .
> Wise, quoted in Joseph B. Felt, "Political Affairs," *History of Ipswich, Essex, and Hamilton* (Cambridge, Mass., 1834, reprinted in Ipswich, Mass.: The Clamshell Press, 1966), 123–25.

I have faced during my life . . . .
> Du Bois, "The Trial," *Writings* (Library of America), 1071. Du Bois, *The Autobiography of W. E. B. Du Bois: A Soliloquy on Viewing My Life from the Last Decade of Its First Century* (New York: International Publishers, 1986), 186.

Free Enterprise

I found you were gone, by accident, . . .
> Dickinson, "To Thomas Wentworth Higginson, Feb 1863," *Letters, Vol. II,* 423–24.

Americans don't own their high standard of living, . . .
> Stein, *Yank—The Army Weekly* (Continental Edition), November 11, 1945. Quoted in *Gertrude Stein's America*, 81.

We peddle, we truck, we sail, we row, . . .
> Emerson, "Emancipation in the British West Indies," *Works XI* (1883), 152–53.

When the ordinary American hears . . . .
> James, "To H. G. Wells, 1906," *Letters, Vol. II*, 260. Quoted in Barzun, *A Stroll with William James*, 218.

The real wealth of the Nation lies . . . .
> Carson, "Letter to *The Washington Post*, Aug 1953," reprinted in *Reader's Digest*, August 1953. Quoted in Brooks, *The House of Life*, 154–55.

Strange it is, however, . . .
> Bailey, *The Holy Earth*, 19–20. Quoted in Andrew Denny Rodgers III, *Liberty Hyde Bailey: A Story of American Plant Sciences* (New York: Hafner Publishing, 1965), 409.

This afternoon, being on Fair Haven Hill, . . .
> Thoreau, "Dec 30 1851," *Selected Journals*, 143–44.

Since we have written you, . . .
> Dickinson, "To Austin Dickinson, Feb 6 1852," *Letters, Vol. I*, 173.

Free Speech

Those things most listened for, . . .
> Whitman, "Letter to Ralph Waldo Emerson (1856)," *Poetry and Prose* (Library of America), 1321.

The Unbelief of the age is attested by . . . .
> Emerson, "Jun 16? 1838," *Emerson in His Journals*, 188.

Personally, I DO NOT LIKE RADIO, . . .
> Hughes, "To Eric Barnouw, Mar 27 1945." Quoted in *Life of Langston Hughes, Vol. II*, 75.

Although mid-twentieth century of the middle ages continued . . . .
> Niedecker, "Untitled," *From This Condensery: The Complete Writing of Lorine Niedecker*, Robert J. Bertholf ed. (Highlands, N.C.: The Jargon Society, 1985), 281.

There is much in life and there is much in art . . . .
> Moore, *The Dial*, 81 (Sep 1926), *The Complete Prose*, 172.

Free Trade

A man coquetting with too many countries . . . .
> James, "To C. E. Norton, Jun 26 1901," *Letters, Vol. II*, 152,

quoted in Perry, *The Thought and Character of William James: Briefer Version*, 249.

The Future

All we know is that it will change, . . .
Ashbery, "Willem de Kooning," *Reported Sightings*, 187.

Generation Gap

I would have been hailed with approval . . . .
Du Bois, quoted in John Edgar Wideman, "Introduction" to Du Bois, *The Souls of Black Folk* (New York: Vintage/The Library of America, 1990), xi.
"The Classics," "the Classics"! . . .
Emerson, "The Protest," *The Early Lectures of Ralph Waldo Emerson, Vol. III*, 88.
Age and youth are great flatterers. . . .
Williams, "Prologue to *Kora in Hell*," *Imaginations*, 19.
We do not think enough of the Dead . . . .
Dickinson, "Prose Fragment 50," *Letters, Vol. III*, 919–20.
Our understanding of human relations . . . .
Moore, "Henry James as a Characteristic American," *The Complete Prose*, 318.
And so I do know what a genius is, . . .
Stein, *Everybody's Autobiography* (New York: Vintage, 1973), 121.

Global Village

And in proportion as a man . . . .
Williams, "Contact," *Selected Essays*, 28.

Golden Rule

For I suppose that liberty . . . .
Emerson, "The Fugitive Slave Law," *Works XI* (1883), 216–17.

Habits of the Heart

The manners of young men . . . .
Emerson, "Nov 18, 1838," *Emerson in His Journals*, 211.
Of Miss P—I know but this, dear. . . .
Dickinson, "To Louise Norcross, late 1872," *Letters, Vol. II*, 500.

Hidden Agenda

What umpire can there be between us . . . .
> James, *Collected Essays and Reviews* (New York: Longmans, 1920), 61, quoted in Barzun, *A Stroll with William James*, 27.

The beginnings are slow and infirm, . . .
> Emerson, "The Sovereignty of Ethics," *The Works of Ralph Waldo Emerson, Vol. X: Lectures and Biographical Sketches* (Boston: Houghton Mifflin/Riverside Press, 1883), 180–81.

Higher Education

If it were possible for every person . . . .
> Bailey, *The Holy Earth*, 50. Quoted in Rodgers, *Liberty Hyde Bailey*, 413.

High Tech

What a Hazard a Letter is! . . .
> Dickinson, "To T. W. Higginson, Aug 6 1885," *Letters, Vol. III*, 884.

History

Let us start at the bottom. . . .
> Stevens, "To Hi Simons, Aug 10 1940," *Letters*, 364.

Only Nature has a right to grieve perpetually, . . .
> Thoreau, "To Mrs. L. C. B., Mar 2 1842," *Letters to Various Persons*, 10.

Home

It hath been always observed here, . . .
> Winthrop, "Feb 10 1631," *Journal*, in *The American Puritans*, 38.

After all anybody is as their land and air is. . . .
> Stein, *What Are Masterpieces* (Los Angeles: The Conference Press, 1940), 62. Quoted in *Gertrude Stein's America*, 45.

Had I not heard as a child . . . .
> Hughes, "Acceptance of the Springarn Medal, NAACP, Jun 26 1960." Quoted in *Life of Langston Hughes, Vol. II*, 312–13.

They say that "home is where the heart is." . . .
> Dickinson, "To Mrs. J. G. Holland, about Jan 20 1856," *Letters, Vol. II*, 324.

There is a commonplace beauty . . . .
> Ives, "The Alcotts," *Essays Before a Sonata*, Howard Boatwright ed. (New York: Norton Library, 1970), 47.

Life is an affair of people not of places. . . .
>Stevens, "Adagia," *Opus Posthumous*, 158.

Home II

We have as good right, . . .
>Emerson, "Considerations by the Way," *Essays and Lectures* (New York: Library of America, 1983), 1082.

How To Be Your Own Best Friend

Take for granted that you've got a temperament . . . .
>James, "To Thomas W. Ward, Jan 1868," *The Selected Letters* (Hardwick ed.), 51.

If you have no faith . . . .
>Emerson, "Courage," *Society and Solitude* (Boston: Fields, Osgood, & Co., 1870), 261.

Is not the sweet resentment . . . .
>Dickinson, "To Mrs. James S. Cooper, Oct 1880," *Letters, Vol. III*, 679.

Talent, knowledge, humility, reverence, . . .
>Moore, "Profit Is a Dead Weight," *The Complete Prose*, 508–9.

How Writing Is Written

Tell children what you say about writing & laboring . . . .
>Emerson, "May 1846," *Emerson in His Journals*, 355.

The sense of strangeness, may we say, . . .
>Moore, "If a Man Die," *The Complete Prose*, 283.

As at all times I write practically every day . . . .
>Stein, "Portraits and Repetition," *Lectures in America*, 200.

The important thing is not to get discouraged . . . .
>Schuyler, "Schuyler in Conversation," *XXIst Century*, I:1, 44.

So far in this world, only my writing . . . .
>Hughes, "To Mrs. R. O. Mason [draft], Jun 6 1930," in *Life of Langston Hughes, Vol. I*, 184.

On days when I want to write . . . .
>Ashbery, "The Art of Poetry XXXIII," Peter Stitt int., *The Paris Review*, no. 90 (Winter 1983), 52.

The length of his walk . . . .
>Emerson, "Thoreau," *Works X* (1883), 431.

One of the essential conditions . . . .
>Stevens, "To Ronald Lane Latimer, Jan 8 1935," *Letters of Wallace Stevens*, 274.

Human Nature

Nature, last week, including human nature. . . .

Niedecker, "To Louis Zukofsky, Jun 6 1948," in Penberthy, *Niedecker and the Correspondence with Zukofsky*, 148–49.

In a civilization like ours, . . .

Jeffers, "To Rudolph Gilbert, Nov 1929," *Selected Letters*, 159–60.

The men, though young, . . .

Emerson, "Nature," *Essays: Second Series*, in *Essays and Lectures* (Library of America), 547.

The killdeer still sitting . . . .

Niedecker, "To Louis Zukofsky, Jun 22 [1948]," *Niedecker and the Correspondence with Zukofsky*, 151.

Immortality

To have been immortal . . . .

Dickinson, "To T. W. Higginson, Jul 1875," *Letters, Vol. II*, 542.

I think we may be sure that, . . .

Emerson [to his son Edward], quoted in John McAleer, *Ralph Waldo Emerson: Days of Encounter* (Boston: Little, Brown, 1984), 656.

Independence Day

England. We use her language, and receive, . . .

Fuller, "American Literature; Its Position in the Present Time, and Prospects for the Future," in *The American Transcendentalists*, 190.

American literature all the nineteenth century . . . .

Stein, "What Is English Literature," *Lectures in America*, 45.

Information Highway

If you chance to live and move . . . .

Thoreau, "Life without Principle," *Thoreau's Vision: The Major Essays*, 187–88.

Inner Resource

In a few days I go to lake Huron, . . .

Whitman, *Specimen Days* (Godine), 100. Also *Poetry and Prose* (Library of America), 880.

If we believed in the existence . . . .

Emerson, "The Heart," *Early Lectures of Ralph Waldo Emerson, Vol. II: 1836–1838*, Stephen E. Whicher, Robert E. Spiller, Wallace E. Williams eds. (Cambridge: Harvard/Belknap, 1964), 285.

Innocents Abroad

When much in the Woods . . . .
    Dickinson, "To T. W. Higginson, Aug 1862," *Letters, Vol. II,* 415.

Invisible Hand

There arose a sudden gust . . . .
    Winthrop, "Journal: Jul 5, 1643," in *The American Puritans,* 43.

Isotropic Universe

All fundamental aspects of anything— . . .
    Ives, "The Amount To Carry," *Essays Before a Sonata,* 240.
In town I also talked with Sampson Reed, . . .
    Emerson, "Jun–Jul 1842," *Emerson in His Journals,* 286.

It's a Wonderful Life

You may open a road, . . .
    James, "To Thomas W. Ward, Jan 1868," *The Selected Letters*
    (Hardwick ed.), 54–55.

Kingdom of Heaven

Nothing is so resonant with mystery . . . .
    Dickinson, "Prose Fragment 925," *Letters, Vol. III,* 926.

Land beside a House

Hope and the future for me . . . .
    Thoreau, "The Wild," *Thoreau's Vision: The Major Essays,* 145–46.

Land Ethic

You say you "feel strongly . . . .
    Fairfield Porter, "Letters to Claire and Robert White," *Parenthèse,*
    No. 4, 212.
Chief Sleepy Eyes . . . .
    Niedecker, "Notes, sec. XI" (unpublished notes attached to notes
    titled "Lake Superior Country: vacation trip '66," 1966), 5. By
    permission of Cid Corman as Literary Executor for the Estate of
    Lorine Niedecker.
I saw the Sacs & Foxes . . . .
    Emerson, "Nov 2 1837," *Emerson in His Journals,* 175.

Library of America

When Flowers annually died . . . .
    Dickinson, "To T. W. Higginson, early 1877," *Letters, Vol. II,* 573.

Life Studies

My own autobiography . . . .

Ashbery, "An Interview with John Ashbery," Sue Gangel int., *San Francisco Review of Books,* November, 1977, 8.

Literary Theory

You cannot imagine the size of a place like Arizona . . . .

Stevens, "To Thomas McGreevy, Mar 11 1949," *Letters of Wallace Stevens,* 632.

I cannot divest my appetite of literature, . . .

Whitman, "Final Confessions—Literary Tests," *Specimen Days* (Godine), 120.

May: 12, Niedecker; *23,* Fuller; *25,* Emerson; *27,* Carson; *31,* Whitman; *Jun: 10,* Porter; *Jul: 12,* Thoreau; *28,* Ashbery; *Aug: 15,* Wise; *Sep: 17,* Williams; *Oct: 2,* Stevens; *5,* Edwards; *20,* Ives; *Nov: 9,* Schuyler; *15,* Moore; *Dec: 10,* Dickinson; *Jan: 10,* Jeffers; *11,* Wm. James; Leopold; *Feb: 1,* Hughes; *3,* Stein; *23,* Du Bois; *Mar: 15,* Bailey.

We have much that we call nature poetry, . . .

Bailey, "An Evolutionist's View of Nature and Religion," *The Independent,* February 2, 1899. Quoted in Rodgers, *Liberty Hyde Bailey,* 349.

Love

If you saw a bullet hit a Bird— . . .

Dickinson, "To recipient unknown [Master], about 1861," *Letters, Vol. II,* 373.

And now another friendship has ended. . . .

Thoreau, "Feb 8 1857," *Selected Journals,* 253.

I could better have the earth taken . . . .

Thoreau, "Feb 8 1857," *Selected Journals,* 253.

Yet Tenderness has not a Date— . . .

Dickinson, "To Otis P. Lord, Apr 30 1882," *Letters, Vol. III,* 728.

Love It or Leave It

I am sitting in a 60-mile-an-hour bus . . . .

Leopold, "Sketches Here and There," *A Sand County Almanac,* 117–18.

Majority Rule

Dear friends—we cannot believe . . . .

Dickinson, "To Mrs. J. G. Holland, Jun 1878," *Letters, Vol. II,* 612.

The Making of Americans

The whole object of the universe . . . .
> Emerson, "undated, 1828," Bliss Perry ed., *The Heart of Emerson's Journals* (Cambridge, Mass.: Houghton Mifflin/The Riverside Press, 1926), 39.

It [culture] must have for its spinal meaning . . . .
> Whitman, "Democratic Vistas," *Poetry and Prose* (Library of America), 962.

In a great many educations in a great many countries . . . .
> Stein, "American Education and College," *How Writing Is Written*, 95.

Manifest Destiny

The evolution-conception of the universe . . . .
> Bailey, *The Outlook to Nature*. Quoted in Rodgers, *Liberty Hyde Bailey*, 348.

As for compliments, even the stars . . . .
> Thoreau, "To Mr. [Harrison Gray Otis] B[lake]., Mar 13 1856," *Letters to Various Persons*, 135.

"I have fallen in love outward" [means] the feeling— . . .
> Jeffers, during a poetry reading at Harvard University, 1941. Quoted in Robert Hass, "Introduction," *Rock and Hawk: A Selection of Shorter Poems by Robinson Jeffers* (New York: Random House, 1987), xxxiii.

There is nothing between us . . . .
> Emerson, "Feb 16 1827," *Emerson in His Journals*, 62.

Materials and Methods

Odd as it may seem that a few words . . . .
> Moore, "Idiosyncrasy and Technique," *The Complete Prose*, 512.

The Media

Remember Sojourner Truth, . . .
> Niedecker, "To Louis Zukofsky, [Jul] 4 [1948]," in Penberthy, *Niedecker and the Correspondence with Zukofsky, 1931–1970*, 152.

It is difficult to believe but it is true, . . .
> Stein, "I Came and Here I Am," *How Writing Is Written*, 71–72.

A camera! a camera! . . .
> Emerson, "Oct 21 1841," quoted in *The Early Lectures of Ralph Waldo Emerson, Vol. III*, 339, and in part in *Emerson in His Journals*, 268.

Modern Times

Passionless and fixed, at the six-stroke the boats come in; . . .
> Whitman, quoted in Justin Kaplan, *Walt Whitman: A Life* (New York: Simon and Schuster, 1980), 111.

The Mother of Us All

Nature is lush here, . . .
> Niedecker, "To Kenneth Cox, Dec 10 1966," in "Extracts from Letters to Kenneth Cox," *The Full Note: Lorine Niedecker* (Budleigh Salterton, Devon: Interim Press, 1983), 36.

We were walking along the beach . . . .
> Schuyler, "Schuyler in Conversation," *XXIst Century* (Winter 1991/1992), 48.

Is it not a bit beside the point . . . .
> Leopold, "Wilderness as a Form of Land Use," *Journal of Land and Public Utility Economics,* I (1925), 401. Quoted in Roderick Nash, *Wilderness and the American Mind* (New Haven: Yale University Press, 1973), 188.

National Endowment

An American Protestant, . . .
> Porter, "Homer," *Art in Its Own Terms: Selected Criticism 1935–1975,* Rackstraw Downes ed. (New York: Taplinger Publishing Company, 1979), 197–98.

National Guard

Fellow Citizens, in these times full of the fate of the Republic, . . .
> Emerson, "Affairs in Kansas," *Works XI: Miscellanies* (1883), 248.

As a group of citizens calling to our country . . . .
> James, "Address on the Philippine Question," *Writings: 1902–1910* (New York: Library of America, 1987), 1135.

Native Tongue

Prospecting thus the coming unsped days, . . .
> Whitman, "Democratic Vistas," *Poetry and Prose* (Library of America), 992.

Clarity is of no importance . . . .
> Stein, "Henry James," *Four in America* (New Haven: Yale, 1947), 127. Quoted in Patricia Meyerowitz, "Introduction to the Dover Edition," *How To Write* (New York: Dover, 1975), xxv.

Sometimes, when I am writing a thing, . . .
> Stevens, "To Hi Simons, Feb 18 1942," *Letters,* 403.

The notes hold into the next general thought, . . .

> Ives, "Memos About the *Concord Sonata* (1913–1929)," *Memos,*
> John Kirkpatrick ed. (London: Calder & Boyars, 1973), 188–89.

Things are in a continual state of motion . . . .

> Ashbery, "The Art of Poetry," *The Paris Review,* No. 90, 46.

The following principles . . . are aids to composition . . . .

> Moore, "Feeling and Precision," *The Complete Prose,* 396.

Tongue II

America is funny that way . . . .

> Stein, *Everybody's Autobiography,* 277.

Natural Law

The idea of right exists in the human mind, . . .

> Emerson, "The Sovereignty of Ethics," *The Works of Ralph Waldo
> Emerson, Vol. X: Lectures and Biographical Sketches* (Boston: Hough-
> ton Mifflin/Riverside Press, 1883), 185–86.

A thing is right when it tends . . . .

> Leopold, "The Land Ethic," *A Sand County Almanac,* 224–25.

Nature

How many animals birds wild flowers . . . .

> Stein, *The Geographical History of America* (New York: Vintage,
> 1973), 69.

New York

I very frequently used to retire . . . .

> Edwards, "Personal Narrative," *Norton Anthology of American Lit-
> erature, Vol. I,* 213.

There is no thrill in all the world . . . .

> Hughes, quoted in *Life of Langston Hughes, Vol. I,* 5.

New York is the focus, . . .

> Fuller, quoted in Perry Miller ed., *Margaret Fuller, American Ro-
> mantic* (Ithaca, N.Y.: Cornell University Press, 1963), 251.

I wanted to be in New York, . . .

> Whitman, quoted in Horace Traubel, *With Walt Whitman in Cam-
> den, Vol. III* (Boston, 1914), 581–82. Quoted again in Kaplan,
> *Walt Whitman: A Life,* 292.

No: New York is not the world. . . .

> Stevens, "To Barbara Church, Mar 14 1949," *Letters,* 633.

Nothing happens in the city. . . .

> Stein, *Blood on the Dining-Room Floor,* John Herbert Gill ed.
> (Berkeley: Creative Arts Book Company, 1982), 51.

No Ideas but in Things

The child should be taught to understand *things*, . . .
> Edwards, quoted in Sereno E. Dwight, *The Life of President Edwards* (New York, 1830), 30, and in Perry Miller, *Errand into the Wilderness* (Cambridge: Harvard/Belknap, 1956), 177.

Knowledge is the thing you know . . . .
> Stein, *Lectures in America*, 11.

From every point of view, the overwhelming . . . .
> James, *The Principles of Psychology, Vol. I* (New York: Henry Holt, 1904), 479–80, quoted in Barzun, *A Stroll with William James*, 58.

At the very moment when abstract thinking . . . .
> Ashbery, quoted in Lehman, *The Line Forms Here*, 172.

As the attributes of the poets of the kosmos concentre . . . .
> Whitman, "1855 Preface," *Poetry and Prose* (Library of America), 18.

And I realized after such a long acquaintanceship . . . .
> Ashbery, "Fairfield Porter," *Reported Sightings*, 314.

A deep insight will always, . . .
> Emerson, "Poetry and Imagination," in *Letters and Social Aims* (Boston: James R. Osgood and Company, 1876), 16.

Lost in Translation*

It hardly required much power of mind to see. . . .
> Donald Davie, "A Demurral," *The New Republic*, April 20, 1987, 38.

The One Thing that Can Save America

The true gravitation-hold of liberalism . . . .
> Whitman, "Democratic Vistas," *Poetry and Prose* (Library of America), 950–51.

G.I.s and G.I.s and G.I.s . . . .
> Stein, *Brewsie and Willie* (New York: Random House, 1946), 113–14.

Early maps with emphasized shore-lines . . . .
> Moore, "from *The Dial*, Aug 1928," *The Complete Prose*, 199.

---

*We must think things, not words.
—Oliver Wendell Holmes, Jr., quoted in Catherine Drinken Bowen, *Yankee from Olympus* (1944), and subsequently in *The Harper Book of American Quotations* (New York: Harper & Row, 1988), 431.

Original Intent

If the Bill of Rights . . . .
> Carson, *Silent Spring* (Boston: Riverside Press/Houghton Mifflin, 1962), 12–13, as quoted in Brooks, *The House of Life*, 276.

Do you suppose the world is finished, . . .
> Whitman, "Other Notebooks, &c. on Words," *Daybooks and Notebooks, Vol. III*, 771.

Original Position

Till it has loved— . . .
> Dickinson, "To T. W. Higginson, Dec 1878," *Letters, Vol. II*, 628.

Over There

After all, would one really go to Europe . . . .
> Stevens, "To Thomas McGreevy, Aug 25 1950," *Letters*, 691.

Our people creep abroad . . . .
> Emerson, "Sep–Nov 1843," *Emerson in His Journals*, 317.

Pair Bond

I have discovered that the thrill . . . .
> Williams, "Prologue to *Kora in Hell*," *Imaginations*, 22, and in *Selected Essays*, 19.

Mrs. Stevens and I went out for a walk . . . .
> Stevens, quoted in Peter Brazeau, *Parts of a World: Wallace Stevens Remembered—An Oral Biography* (New York: Random House, 1983), 43. Quoted as epigraph to John Koethe, "Contrary Impulses: The Tension between Poetry and Theory," *Critical Inquiry* 18, (Autumn 1991), 64.

Patriotic Songs

We have had two peerless summer days . . . .
> Emerson, "May 31 1837," *Emerson in His Journals*, 165.

And when all is still at night, the owls . . . .
> Thoreau, "Aug 1845" [*Journals*], reprinted in *The Annotated Walden*, 255.

Pledge of Allegiance

This is what you shall do: . . .
> Whitman, "Preface to *Leaves of Grass* (1855)," *Poetry and Prose* (Library of America), 11.

Poetry

This is a time for the highest poetry. . . .
> Stevens, "To Rolfe Fjelde (Yale Literary Magazine), Apr 16 1946," *Letters*, 526.

Poetry II

Will it help breed one . . . .
> Whitman, "Preface (1855)," *Poetry and Prose* (Library of America), 26.

Poetry and Prose

If I read a book it makes my whole body. . . .
> Dickinson, quoted by Higginson after their first encounter, Aug 16 1870, in *Letters, Vol. II*, 473–74. Also quoted in Sewall, *Life of Emily Dickinson, Vol. II*, 566.

Is not poetry the little chamber in the brain . . . .
> Emerson, "Poetry and Imagination," *Letters and Social Aims*, 57.

What is poetry and if you know . . . .
> Stein, "Poetry and Grammar," *Lectures in America*, 209.

Poetry is a magic of pauses, . . .
> Moore, "Poetry and Criticism," *The Complete Prose*, 589.

It is conceivable that what is unified form . . . .
> Ives, "Emerson," *Essays Before a Sonata*, 23.

A friend of mine, Arthur Gold, . . .
> Schuyler, "An Interview by Mark Hillringhouse," *American Poetry Review*, 14, no. 2 (March/April, 1985), 12.

I find one can say very much more . . . .
> Ashbery, "Craft Interview with John Ashbery," William Packard int., *The Craft of Poetry* (Garden City, N.Y.: Doubleday, 1974), 118.

All the interest that you feel . . . .
> Stevens, "To José Rodríguez Feo, Jan 26 1945," *Letters*, 485.

Poetry Reading

It is not easy to appear spiritual . . . .
> Hughes, "To Colson Leigh, Inc., Oct 12 1946," quoted in *Life of Langston Hughes, Vol. II*, 97.

Profiles in Courage

There are communities—now partly vanished, . . .*
> Ives, "Epilogue," *Essays Before a Sonata,* 101.

Sam Patch

In his late teens, Patch gained local fame . . . .
> Henry W. Clune, *The Genesee* (New York: Holt, Rinehart and Winston, 1963), 236–38.

In defiance of fate . . . .
> W.P.A. Guide, *Rochester and Monroe County,* 93.

---

*HIGH FALLS in the Brown's Race Historic District of Downtown Rochester, N.Y. ·Outdoor Laser, Light & Sound Spectacular ·The drama unfolds as a Seneca Indian spirit tells her tale about people and the gorge to a young bear whose grandad leaped with daredevil Sam Patch on his ill-fated jump off the High Falls in 1829. . . . [n.] onto State Street; right onto Platt Street.
—*Rochester Riverside Convention Center* (716-232-7200), Rochester, N.Y. 14604.

Battle Creek. In OAK HILL CEMETERY, South Ave. and Hussey St., is the Grave of Sojourner Truth. The grave, in the cemetery's Fifth Street, is marked by an old-fashioned square monument. . . . A few days before her death in 1883, she said: "I isn't goin' to die, honey, I'se goin' home like a shootin' star."
—W.P.A., *Michigan: A Guide to the Wolverine State,* 195–97.

IPSWICH, 11.7 *m.* The Rebellion Tablet marks the spot where in 1687 the townsfolk, led by John Wise, gathered nearly 100 years before the Revolution in angry protest against the oppression of Governor Andros.
—W.P.A., Federal Writers' Program. *The WPA Guide to Massachusetts* (New York: Pantheon, 1983), 417.

Proceed on Route 133 . . . watch [n. of Essex] for an historic marker in front of a dark clapboard house. John Wise, the first pastor of the first church in Chebacco Parish, built this house in the open farmland about 1710.
—The Junior League of Boston, *Along the Coast of Essex County: A Guidebook,* introduction by Richard W. Hale Jr. (Amesbury, Mass.: Essex County Tourist Council, 1970), 140.

"And who was Sam Patch?" . . .

> William Dean Howells, *Their Wedding Journey* (1871). Quoted in
> W.P.A. Guide, *Rochester and Monroe County*, 9.

Sojourner Truth

Born sometime shortly after 1790, . . .

> Federal Writers' Program, W.P.A. Guide, *Michigan: A Guide to the
> Wolverine State* (New York: Oxford University Press, 1941), 195.

"I will speak upon the ashes," she said . . . .*

> Larry B. Massie and Peter J. Schmitt, *Battle Creek: The Place Be-
> hind the Products* (Woodland Hills, Calif.: Windsor Publications,
> 1984), 27.

A series of women's conventions . . . .

> Howard Zinn, *A People's History of the United States* (New York:
> Harper & Row, 1980), 122.

John Wise

A boat's crew from his parish . . . .

> Joseph B. Felt, *History of Ipswich, Essex, and Hamilton, Mass.*, (Cam-
> bridge, 1834), reprinted (Ipswich, Mass.: The Clamshell Press,
> 1966), 259.

Perhaps the reason for his uniqueness . . . .

> Miller, *The American Puritans*, 121.

1770—Boston Massacre. *1772*—Rev. John Wise's famous "Vindica-
tion . . . .

> Elizabeth H. Newton, Alice Keenan, and Mary P. Conley, *Three
> Hundred & Fifty Years of Ipswich History* (Ipswich, Mass.: The
> Three Hundred and Fiftieth Anniversary Committee of the
> Town of Ipswich, 1984), 7–8.

---

*She often spoke in parables. In the early 1850s, after passage of the
Fugitive Slave Law, there was a strong division between the
Freesoilers, who advocated freedom for slaves but with limitation,
and Garrison's followers who sought to abolish slavery. Sojourner
said she could not explain very clearly the difference between
Freesoilers and Garrisonians but she could *feel* the difference. "I
remember seeing folks hackle flax," she said in her deep resonant
voice. "Some worked by—the—day, by—the—day, and others
worked by the job, by the job, by the job, job, job. Freesoilers work
by—the—day but the Garrisonians work by the job, job, job."
—Berenice Bryant Lowe, *Tales of Battle Creek* (Battle Creek, Mich.:
Albert L. and Louise B. Miller Foundation, 1976), 239–40.

Why does one not hear Americans speak . . . .
> Williams, "Père Sebastian Rasles," *In the American Grain* (New York: New Directions, 1956), 113.

The Public and Its Problems

It is the fashion of a certain set to despise "politics" . . . .
> Whitman, Brooklyn *Eagle* editorial, quoted in Zweig, *Walt Whitman: The Making of the Poet* (New York: Basic Books, 1984), 31.

We were proud of the people . . . .
> Emerson, "To Thomas Carlyle, Jan 7 1866," *The Correspondence of Thomas Carlyle and Ralph Waldo Emerson, 1834–1872, Vol. I,* Charles Eliot Norton ed. (Boston: James R. Osgood and Company, 1883), 296–97.

Those of us engaged in this racial struggle . . . .
> Hughes, "The Fun of Being Black," *The Langston Hughes Reader* (New York: George Braziller, Inc., 1958), 500.

Publish or Perish

To those to whom we owe affection, . . .
> Emerson, "To Thomas Carlyle, Mar 11 1854," *The Correspondence of Thomas Carlyle and Ralph Waldo Emerson, Vol. I,* 231.

Had we less to say to those we love, . . .
> Dickinson, "To Louise and Frances Norcross, Jan 14 1885," *Letters, Vol. III,* 855.

Pursuit of Happiness

Life consists in . . . .
> Emerson, "Aug 1847," *Emerson in His Journals,* 377.

Naturally if you want to sell things . . . .
> Stein, "American Education and Colleges," *How Writing Is Written,* 98.

To live in Cuba, to think a little . . . .
> Stevens, "To José Rodríguez Feo, Jun 20 1945," *Letters,* 505–6.

Ambiguity seems to be the same thing . . . .
> Ashbery, "The Art of Poetry," *The Paris Review,* no. 90, 45–46.

Quiet Desperation

Of course I know, as well as anybody . . . .
> James, "To Wincenty Lutoslawski, Aug 18 1899," quoted in Ralph Barton Perry, *The Thought and Character of William James, Vol. II* (Boston: Little, Brown, 1935), 272, and partly in Perry, *The Thought and Character of William James, Briefer Version,* 225.

How is one to restore savor to life . . . .
Stevens, "To Barbara Church, Sep 15 1948," *Letters*, 615.

Readers' Guide

It may be true that the author's revisions . . . .
Moore, "The Cantos," *The Complete Prose of Marianne Moore*, 273.
I'm all right [ ]. . . .
Niedecker, "To Louis Zukofsky, Mar 19 1956," *Sulfur* 18, 130;
and in Penberthy, *Niedecker and the Correspondence with Zukofsky*,
226. The empty brackets are Niedecker's.
I'm really much more of a reader. . . .
Schuyler, in Carl Little, "An Interview with James Schuyler,"
Agni 37 (1993), 176.
The only poems I liked as a child . . . .
Hughes, *The Big Sea*, in *The Langston Hughes Reader*, 332.
I am glad there are Books. . . .
Dickinson, "To F. B. Sanborn, about 1873," *Letters, Vol. II*, 516.

Right to Life

If Government knew how, . . .
Emerson, "Oct? 1852," *Emerson in His Journals*, 439.
If nobody had to die . . . .
Stein, *The Geographical History of America* (New York: Vintage,
1973), 53.
I am saving a Miller . . . .
Dickinson, "To Edward (Ned) Dickinson, autumn 1873," *Letters,
Vol. II*, 513.

Right to Privacy

Cannot we let people be themselves, . . .
Emerson, "Education," *Works X* (1883), 136.
A private life is the long thick tree . . . .
Stein, "The Gradual Making of *The Making of Americans*," *Lectures in America*, 155.
The zoo shows us that privacy . . . .
Moore, "What There Is To See at the Zoo," *The Complete Prose*,
475.

Saving Grace

The artist can profitably forgo . . . .
Porter, "Against Idealism," *Art in Its Own Terms*, 106.

Experience in its immediacy . . . .

> James, "The Thing and Its Relations," *Writings, 1902–1910* (New York: Library of America, 1987), 782.

School of Thought

Q: What is Transcendentalism, Mr. Emerson? . . .

> Emerson, quoted in Charles J. Woodbury, *Talks with Ralph Waldo Emerson* (New York: The Baker & Taylor Co., 1890), 108.

Secret Ingredient

The inadequacy of the work . . . .

> Emerson, "Lecture on the Times," *Essays & Lectures* (Library of America), 165.

Self-Portrait

As every man has his hobby-liking, . . .

> Whitman, "Entering a Long Farm Lane," *Specimen Days* (Godine), 61. Also *Poetry and Prose* (Library of America), 781.

Self-Reliance

No matter how complicated anything is, . . .

> Stein, "Portraits and Repetition," *Lectures in America*, 179–80.

Now as well as I can describe it, . . .

> James, "To Mrs. James, 1878," *The Selected Letters* (Hardwick ed.), 109.

It must often have occurred to Pollock . . . .

> Ashbery, "The Invisible Avant-Garde," *Reported Sightings*, 390–91.

Guile permits a lion . . . .

> Hughes, *Chicago Defender*, Oct 29 1945. Quoted in *Life of Langston Hughes, Vol. II*, 121.

Do not try to be saved— . . .

> Dickinson, "To Thomas Wentworth Higginson, Sep 1877," *Letters, Vol. II*, 594.

There is something in my nature *furtive* . . . .

> Whitman, quoted in Kaplan, *Walt Whitman: A Life*, 18.

The thing one gradually comes to find out . . . .

> Stein, *What Are Master-pieces* (p. 84) quoted in Patricia Meyerowitz, "Introduction" to Stein, *How To Write*, xi.

But why I changed? Why I left . . . .

> Thoreau, "Jan 22 1852" *[Journals]*, quoted in *The Annotated Walden*, 88.

To summarize: Humility is an indispensable ally, . . .
> Moore, "Humility, Concentration, and Gusto," *The Complete Prose*, 426.

Sex to Sex*

I sometimes remember we are to die, ...
> Dickinson, "To Susan Gilbert Dickinson, about 1883," *Letters, Vol. III*, 792.

Why as I just look in the railroad car . . . .
> Whitman, "Other Notebooks, &c. on Words," *Daybooks and Notebooks, Vol. III*, 764–65.

From the necessity of loving . . . .
> Emerson, "Thoughts on Modern Literature," *Essays and Lectures* (Library of America), 1166.

Small Planet

This world is just a little place, . . .
> Dickinson, "To Louise and Frances Norcross, mid-Sep 1860," *Letters, Vol. II*, 368.

Society and Solitude

Why leave the place where life is— . . .
> Hughes, *Chicago Defender*, Jan 8 1966. Quoted in *Life of Langston Hughes, Vol. II*, 396.

I cannot get enough alone . . . .
> Emerson, "July 1849," *Emerson in His Journals*, 401.

I can't enter into social meetings . . . .
> Niedecker, "To Cid Corman, Oct 13 1966," *"Between Your House and Mine,"* 102.

There's nobody I'd rather meet; but . . . .
> Jeffers, "To Albert Bender, Jun 1927," *The Selected Letters*, 112–13.

Another ring at the door— . . .
> Dickinson, "To Austin Dickinson, Mar 2 1852," *Letters, Vol. I*, 185–86.

This spring I have had quite a number of invitations . . . .
> Stevens, "To Barbara Church, Jul 17 1950," *Letters of Wallace Stevens*, 684.

---

*Sex to sex, and even to odd;—
—Ralph Waldo Emerson, "Ode, Inscribed to W. H. Channing," quoted by James Schuyler in "The Fauré Ballade," *Hymn to Life* (New York: Random House, 1974), 114.

Some are so inconsiderate as to ask . . . .
    Thoreau, "Aug 31 1856," *Selected Journals*, 244.
Solitude is fearsome & heavy hearted. . . .
    Emerson, "Feb 19 1838," *Emerson in His Journals*, 181.
Sensibility imposes silence . . . .
    Moore, "The World Imagined Since We Are Poor," *The Complete Prose*, 430.

The Songs We Know Best

Women in These States approach the day . . . .
    Whitman, "Letter to Ralph Waldo Emerson," *Poetry and Prose* (Library of America), 1335.
Ives is a great admirer . . . .
    Ives, *Memos*, John Kirkpatrick ed. (London: Calder & Boyars Ltd., 1973), 141n. The words are Ives' own.

Sons and Lovers

Be an opener of doors . . . .
    Emerson, "June? 1844," *Emerson in His Journals*, 328. Also "Jun 15 1844," *The Heart of Emerson's Journals*, 208.

Space Age

I said you see you look up . . . .
    Stein, quoted in *Gertrude Stein's America*, 91–92.
Light blue above, darker below, . . .
    Schuyler, "Jul 8 1969," *For Joe Brainard*, 16–17.
I am always trying to tell this thing . . . .
    Stein, "The Gradual Making of *The Making of Americans*," *Lectures in America*, 160–61.

Spin Control

Life defies our phrases, . . .
    James, original opening paragraph for 1901–1902 Gifford Lectures quoted in Perry, *The Thought and Character of William James: Briefer Version*, 258.
An attitude, physical or mental— . . .
    Moore, in Mary Austin, *Everyman's Genius* (New York: Bobbs Merrill, 1925), 339, and in *The Complete Prose*, 643.
In the last few years I have been trying to keep meaningfulness . . . .
    Ashbery, "Craft Interview with John Ashbery," *The Craft of Poetry*, 121.

A Star Is Born

When the success began and it was a success . . . .
 Stein, "And Now," *How Writing Is Written*, 63.

Supply Side

The merchants and company have long laughed . . . .
 Thoreau, "To Mr. [Harrison Otis] B[lake], Nov 16 1857," *Letters to Various Persons*, 161–62.

Talk Show

Of "shunning Men and Women"— . . .
 Dickinson, "To T. W. Higginson, Aug 1862," *Letters II*, 415.

A Theory of Justice

As the greatest lessons of Nature . . . .
 Whitman, "Democratic Vistas," *Poetry and Prose* (Library of America), 929.
One does not act rightly . . . .
 Bailey, *The Holy Earth*, 3. Quoted in Rodgers, *Liberty Hyde Bailey*, 406.

Things as They Are

The realist thinks he knows . . . .
 Porter, "Art and Knowledge," *Art in Its Own Terms*, 259.
You sometimes charge me . . . .
 Emerson, "To Thomas Carlyle, Feb 29 1844," *The Correspondence of Thomas Carlyle and Ralph Waldo Emerson, 1834–1872, Vol. II*, Charles Eliot Norton ed. (Boston: James R. Osgood and Company, 1883), 59.
Father called to say that our steelyard . . . .
 Dickinson, "To Mrs. J. G. Holland, early Nov 1865," *Letters, Vol. II*, 444.
For nine readers out of ten, . . .
 Stevens, "To Sister M. Bernetta Quinn, May 29 1952," *Letters*, 753.

Thinking like a Mountain

Man is made of the same atoms the world is, . . .
 Emerson, "Worship," *Essays & Lectures* (Library of America), 1075–76.
We are parts in a living sensitive creation. . . .
 Bailey, *The Holy Earth*, 30. Reprinted in Worster, *American Environmentalism*, 231.

You must ascend a mountain to learn . . . .

Thoreau, "To Mr. [Harrison Otis] B[lake], Nov 16 1857," *Letters to Various Persons*, 164–65.*

We have looked first at man . . . .

Carson, "National Book Award Acceptance Speech, 1953," in Brooks, *The House of Life*, 129.

Man is a part of nature, . . .

Jeffers, "To the American Humanist Association, Mar 25 1951," *The Selected Letters*, 342.

For myself, the indefinite, the impersonal, . . .

Stevens, *Sur Plusieurs Beaux Sujects*, Milton J. Bates ed. (Stanford: Stanford University Press, 1989), 33.

Man would be better, more sane . . . .

Jeffers, "To Jack Wilson, Feb 1942," *The Selected Letters*, 291.

The journey of the rock . . . .

Niedecker, "Lake Superior Country, vacation trip '66" (unpublished ms. notes), 1. Quoted in part in my article, "On Lorine Niedecker," *Raritan*, XII, no. 2, 62. By permission of Cid Corman, Literary Executor for the Estate of Lorine Niedecker.

This Land Is Your Land

California is sown thick . . . .

Whitman, *An American Primer*, Horace Traubel ed. (Cambridge: The Cambridge University Press, 1904), 29–30. Whitman, *An American Primer* (Stevens Point, Wis.: Holy Cow! Press, 1987), 29–30.

I think the American Revolution bought . . . .

Emerson, "Affairs in Kansas," *Works XI* (1883), 248.

---

*I now suspect that just as a deer herd lives in mortal fear of its wolves, so does a mountain live in mortal fear of its deer. And perhaps with better cause, for while a buck pulled down by wolves can be replaced in two or three years, a range pulled down by too many deer may fail of replacement in as many decades.

So also with cows. The cowman who cleans his range of wolves does not realize that he is taking over the wolf's job of trimming the herd to fit the range. He has not learned to think like a mountain. Hence we have dustbowls, and rivers washing the future into the sea.

—Aldo Leopold, "Thinking Like a Mountain," *A Sand County Almanac*, 132.

The things that used to be the romantic thing . . . .
    Stein, "American States and Cities and How They Differ from
    Each Other," *How Writing Is Written*, 80.
I looked out the window of the Pullman . . . .
    Hughes, *The Big Sea*, in *The Langston Hughes Reader*, 351–52.
My own country never interested me . . . .
    Ashbery, "An Interview by Ross Labrie," *American Poetry Review*
    (May/June 1984), 29.
Here in Hartford is an exhibition . . . .
    Stevens, "To Thomas McGreevy, Dec 8 1948," *Letters*, 626.

Tradition and the Individual Talent

When the student leader of a prayer meeting . . . .
    Du Bois, *Dusk of Dawn* (Library of America), 594–95.
When a Child and fleeing from Sacrament . . . .
    Dickinson, "To Mrs. J. G. Holland, May 1874," *Letters, Vol. II*,
    524–25.

Twenty-First Century

What are they going to try next, . . .
    Stein, "My Last about Money," *How Writing Is Written*, 112.
Well in a kind of way the American . . . .
    Stein, "The New Hope in Our 'Sad Young Men,' " *How Writing Is
    Written*, 143.

Uncertainty Principle

Life is in the transitions . . . .
    James, "A World of Pure Experience," *The Writings of William
    James*, John J. McDermott ed. (Chicago: University of Chicago
    Press, 1977), 212–13.
Every thing teaches transition, . . .
    Emerson, "Jun 1847," *Emerson in His Journals*, 372.

Vanity Fair

We are suffering from too much sarcasm, . . .
    Moore, "Idiosyncrasy and Technique," *Complete Prose*, 512–13.

Vote with Your Feet

I found Henry T. yesterday in my woods. . . .
    Emerson, "Jan 1858," *Emerson in His Journals*, 480.

War and Peace

In a World too full of Beauty . . . .
    Dickinson, "To Mary Ingersoll Cooper, about 1882," *Letters, Vol. III*, 734.

The Weather

Hard clouds, & hard expressions, & hard manners, I love.
    Emerson, "Sep–Nov 1843," *Emerson in His Journals*, 316.
As for me, I love screaming, wrestling, boiling-hot days.
    Whitman, "Letter to R. W. Emerson (1856)," *Poetry and Prose* (Library of America), 1335.*

Wild Blue Yonder

I always liked boats but . . . .
    Stein, "I Came and Here I Am," *How Writing Is Written*, 70.
What is so good in a college as . . . .
    Emerson, "Nov 14 1865," *Emerson in His Journals*, 531.
Nothing too close, nothing too far off . . . .
    Whitman, "Preface (1855)," *Poetry and Prose* (Library of America), 9.

---

*I like dry light, & hard clouds, hard expressions, & hard manners.
—Ralph Waldo Emerson, "Feb–Mar 1861," *Emerson in His Journals*, 403.

Index

An annoyance by no means petty is the lack of an index.*

Marianne Moore—

---

*An annoyance by no means petty. . . .
—Moore, "The Cantos," *The Complete Prose,* 273.

UNDER DISCUSSION
David Lehman, General Editor
Donald Hall, Founding Editor

Volumes in the Under Discussion series collect reviews and essays about individual poets. The series is concerned with contemporary American and English poets about whom the consensus has not yet been formed and the final vote has not been taken. Titles in the series include:

Printed and bound by CPI Group (UK) Ltd, Croydon, CR0 4YY

13/04/2025

14656538-0001